RELATIVISTIC KINEMATICS

LECTURE NOTES AND SUPPLEMENTS IN PHYSICS

John David Jackson and David Pines, *Editors*

Mathematics for Quantum Mechanics	*John David Jackson (Illinois)*
Elementary Excitations in Solids	*David Pines (Illinois)*
Fundamental Particles	*K. Nishijima (Illinois)*
Matrix Methods in Optical Instrument Design	*Willem Brouwer (Diffraction Limited)*
Relativistic Kinematics	*R. Hagedorn (CERN)*

RELATIVISTIC KINEMATICS

A GUIDE TO THE KINEMATIC PROBLEMS OF HIGH-ENERGY PHYSICS

*

R. HAGEDORN
CERN

1963

THE BENJAMIN/CUMMINGS PUBLISHING COMPANY, INC.

ADVANCED BOOK PROGRAM
Reading, Massachusetts

London · Amsterdam · Don Mills, Ontario · Sydney · Tokyo

RELATIVISTIC KINEMATICS

First printing, 1963
Second printing, with corrections, 1964
Third printing, with corrections, 1973
Fourth printing, 1978

The publisher is pleased to acknowledge the assistance of Zeb Delaire, who composed the volume, and of William Prokos, who produced the artwork and designed the cover.

International Standard Book Numbers
Clothbound: 0–805–33600–1
Paperbound: 0–805–33601–10
Library of Congress Catalog Card Number: 63–21985

Manufactured in the United States of America

ABCDEFGHIJ-DO-798

EDITORS' FOREWORD

Everyone concerned with the teaching of physics at the advanced undergraduate or graduate level is aware of the continuing need for a modernization and reorganization of the basic course material. Despite the existence today of many good textbooks in these areas, there is always an appreciable time-lag in the incorporation of new viewpoints and techniques which result from the most recent developments in physics research. Typically these changes in concepts and material take place first in the personal lecture notes of some of those who teach graduate courses. Eventually, printed notes may appear, and some fraction of such notes evolve into textbooks or monographs. But much of this fresh material remains available only to a very limited audience, to the detriment of all. Our series aims at filling this gap in the literature of physics by presenting occasional volumes with a contemporary approach to the classical topics of physics at the advanced undergraduate and graduate level. Clarity and soundness of treatment will, we hope, mark these volumes, as well as the freshness of the approach.

Another area in which the series hopes to make a contribution is by presenting useful supplementing material of well-defined scope. This may take the form of a survey of relevant mathematical principles, or a collection of reprints of basic papers in a field. Here the aim is to provide the instructor with added flexibility through the use of supplements at relatively low cost.

The scope of both the lecture notes and supplements is somewhat different from the "Frontiers in Physics" series. In spite of wide variations from institution to institution as to what comprises the basic graduate course program, there is a widely accepted group of "bread and butter" courses that deal with the classic topics in physics. These include: Mathematical methods of physics, electromagnetic theory, advanced dynamics, quantum mechanics, statistical mechanics, and frequently nuclear physics and/or solid-state physics. It is chiefly these areas that will be covered by the present series. The listing is perhaps best described as including all advanced undergraduate and graduate courses which are at a level below seminar courses dealing entirely with current research topics.

The publishing format for the series is in keeping with its intentions. Photo-offset printing is used throughout, and the books are paperbound in order to speed publication and reduce costs. It is hoped that books will thereby be within the financial reach of graduate students in this country and abroad.

Finally, because the series represents something of an experiment on the part of the editors and the publisher, suggestions from interested readers as to format, contributors, and contributions will be most welcome.

J. David Jackson
David Pines

PREFACE

This book is a revised version of the author's own lecture notes—except for Chapter 7 (phase-space considerations), which has recently been written expressely for this volume. The lectures were given during the winter of 1961-1962 at CERN, Geneva.

The lectures were not thoroughly planned when they started, and they took, in fact, a course that was by no means anticipated, either by the audience or by the author. The actual course was a kind of Brown's motion, where the author was pushed by the never-ending questions of his listeners into a new direction in about every second lecture. His only trouble was to achieve a reasonable compromise between the diverging forces of the questions and his intention not to leave the frame given by the title of the series.

Thus this book is the result of an agreeable collaboration of many experimental physicists, who know their kinematic's headaches very well, and the author, who sometimes had the aspirin for them. The aim, however, was not so much to cure each individual headache, but rather to give the "know how" to prevent them.

If it should turn out that this book fills a gap between the "high-brow" theory and the daily work in the laboratory, then its purpose will be fully met.

The author and the publisher acknowledge gratefully CERN's permission to publish a former CERN report (CERN 62-18) in this form.

R. Hagedorn

Munich, Germany
August 1963

CONTENTS

1

LORENTZ TRANSFORMATIONS AND INVARIANTS

1-1 THE INVARIANT LINE ELEMENT

It is one of the most important facts of physics that the velocity of light, $c = 2.99793 \cdots \times 10^{10}$ cm/sec, is the same in all inertial systems. This has the consequence that, if light is supposed to be the fastest means of communication, all measurements involving distances must be influenced by this fact. Indeed this influence is expressed by the Lorentz transformations.

Let K and K′ be two reference systems† moving with constant velocity with respect to each other. We call an "event" or a world point the set

$$P \equiv \{xyzt\} \tag{1-1}$$

of space-time coordinates.

Let the directions of the axes of K and K′ be parallel and such that the x and x′ axes coincide and are parallel to the relative velocity (see Fig. 1-1).

Consider two particular events P_1 and P_2 in the frame K, where

$$P_1 \equiv (x_1 y_1 z_1 t_1)$$

is sending out a light signal at time t_1 from the space point $x_1 y_1 z_1$ and

$$P_2 \equiv (x_2 y_2 z_2 t_2)$$

†Frequently called "Lorentz systems."

is receiving this signal at time t_2 in the space point $x_2 y_2 z_2$. The distance between the space points is

$$d = \sqrt{(x_2 - x_1)^2 + (y_2 - y_1)^2 + (z_2 - z_1)^2}$$

but since c is a fixed constant for all inertial systems, it is also given by

$$d = c(t_2 - t_1)$$

Hence

$$(x_2 - x_1)^2 + (y_2 - y_1)^2 + (z_2 - z_1)^2 = c(t_2 - t_1)^2 \qquad (1\text{-}2)$$

But we could have written the same in system K′:

$$(x_2' - x_1')^2 + (y_2' - y_1')^2 + (z_2' - z_1')^2 = c^2(t_2' - t_1')^2 \qquad (1\text{-}2')$$

with the *same* constant c.

We now introduce $\tau \equiv ict$ and go over to infinitesimal distances. We call the square of the distance between any two events which are very near to each other

$$ds^2 = c^2\, dt^2 - dx^2 - dy^2 - dz^2 = -(dx^2 + dy^2 + dz^2 + d\tau^2)$$

and conclude from (1-2) and (1-2′) that

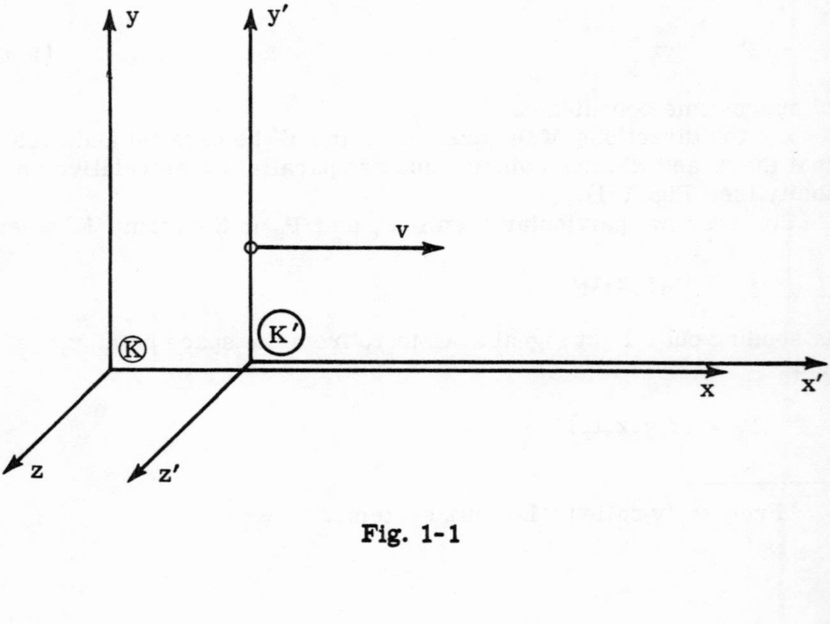

Fig. 1-1

$$ds = 0 \quad \text{implies} \quad ds' = 0 \tag{1-3}$$

As ds and ds′ are of the same order, it follows that $ds = a\, ds'$, and, since K and K′ are on an equal footing, $ds' = a\, ds$; hence $a = \pm 1$ and only $a = +1$ remains for reasons of continuity. By integrating between any two events we see that this is an invariant quantity with respect to the coordinate transformations from K to K′.

$$\underbrace{\int_{P_1}^{P_2} ds = \sqrt{-(\Delta x^2 + \Delta y^2 + \Delta z^2 + \Delta \tau^2)}}_{\text{K system}}$$

$$= \underbrace{\int_{P_1'}^{P_2'} ds' = \sqrt{-(\Delta x'^2 + \Delta y'^2 + \Delta z'^2 + \Delta \tau'^2)}}_{\text{K}' \text{ system}} \tag{1-4}$$

The word *invariant* denotes one of the central ideas of the theory of special relativity, and invariants are a very convenient tool to do calculations. We call $ds^2 = -dx^2 - dy^2 - dz^2 + c^2\, dt^2$ the invariant line element.

1-2 SPACELIKE AND TIMELIKE DISTANCES; FUTURE AND PAST; THE LIGHT CONE

We now ask two questions. Given two events P_1 and P_2 with distance $\{\Delta x, \Delta y, \Delta z, \Delta \tau\}$ is there a system in which these two events appear at the same time? We have then $\Delta \tau' = 0$, but from (1-4) it follows that

$$\Delta s^2 = -(\Delta x^2 + \Delta y^2 + \Delta z^2 + \Delta \tau^2) = -(\Delta x'^2 + \Delta y'^2 + \Delta z'^2) \leq 0$$

Thus

> a system in which two events happen at the same *time* can be found if and only if
>
> $\Delta s^2 = c^2\, \Delta t^2 - \Delta x^2 - \Delta y^2 - \Delta z^2 \leq 0$ (spacelike distance) (1-5)

On the other hand, we ask: Can two events appear to happen at the same place in some system K′? We have then

$$\Delta s^2 = -(\Delta x^2 + \Delta y^2 + \Delta z^2 + \Delta \tau^2)$$
$$= -\Delta\tau'^2 = +c^2\,\Delta t'^2 \geq 0$$

Therefore,

a system in which two events happen at the same *place* can be found if and only if $\Delta s^2 = c^2\,\Delta t^2 - \Delta x^2 - \Delta y^2 - \Delta z^2 \geq 0$ (timelike distance)	(1-6)

Since Δs^2 is invariant, either $\Delta s^2 \geq 0$ in all Lorentz systems or $\Delta s^2 \leq 0$ in all Lorentz systems. We have to add the case $\Delta s^2 = 0$, which applies to the distance between two events connected by a light signal [see (1-2) and (1-2′)].

Consider now all possible events with respect to a given one. Put the coordinate origin into the given event 0: $(x = y = z = t = 0)$ and draw two coordinates (x,t) only (Fig. 1-2).

The distance from the origin is given by the invariant

$$s^2 = c^2t^2 - x^2 - y^2 - z^2$$

(a) $\underline{s^2 = 0}$. Connects all those events with the origin which can be reached by a light signal; hence the cone $s^2 = 0$ is called the "light cone" and these events are said to be on the light cone.

(b) $\underline{s^2 > 0}$. If $s > 0$, the event is in the forward light cone; if $s < 0$, it is in the backward light cone. Clearly an event in the forward light cone appears later as 0, in the backward light cone it appears earlier as 0.

Since s^2 is an invariant, one cannot transform an event with $s < 0$ into one with $s > 0$, since all these transformations form a connected continuous group.

Therefore the forward light cone contains the absolute future, and the backward cone the absolute past. Only events in the backward cone can have an influence on 0, and 0 can have an influence only on events in the forward cone.

(c) $\underline{s^2 < 0}$. Spacelike events; no interaction with 0.

This is how causality is expressed on this level of argument.

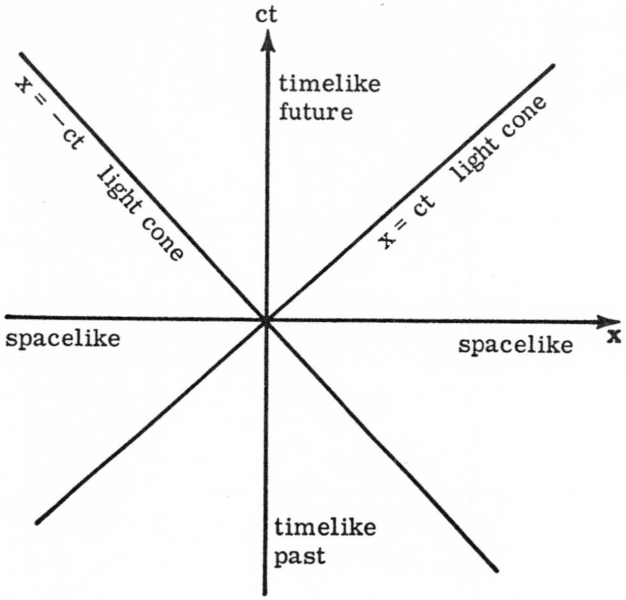

Fig. 1-2 Timelike and spacelike distances; past and future; the light cone.

[*Remark:*
It finds its most direct application in quantum field theory where the measurement of the field at the origin and at a world point $P = \{xyzt\}$ do not interfere, if P lies spacelike. Therefore the two operators corresponding to the fields must commute

$$[A(P_1),A(P_2)] = 0 \qquad \text{if } P_1 \text{ and } P_2 \text{ lie spacelike to each other} \tag{1-7}$$

The dispersion relations are derived from this requirement.]

Problems:

1-1. Define the proper time of a moving body to be the time shown by a clock which moves with that body. Use the invariance of Δs^2 to establish the lifetime of a particle measured by a clock in the lab. system (a) if the particle moves with constant velocity, and (b) if the particle moves arbitrarily.

1-2. Is the light quantum a stable particle?

Solution to 1-1:

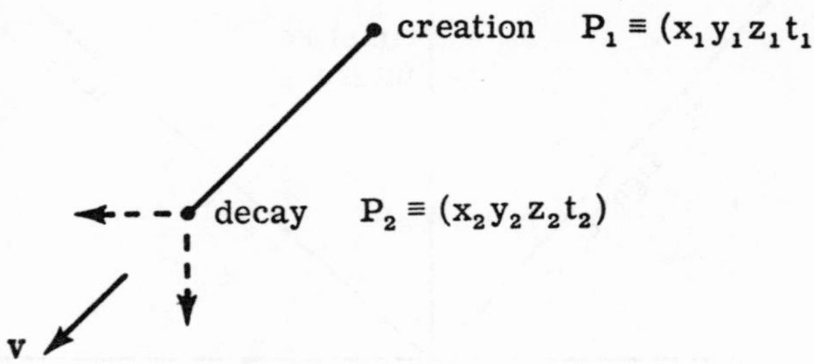

In the lab. system we find the distance between creation and decay $\Delta s^2 = c^2\ \Delta t^2 - \Delta x^2 - \Delta y^2 - \Delta z^2$, but in the particles system $\Delta s^2 = c^2\ \Delta t'^2$, since there it is at rest; Hence

$$\Delta t' = \Delta t \sqrt{1 - \frac{\Delta x^2 + \Delta y^2 + \Delta z^2}{c^2\ \Delta t^2}}$$

$$= \Delta t \sqrt{1 - \beta^2} \qquad \beta \equiv \frac{v}{c}$$

(a) $t_2' - t_1' = (t_2 - t_1)\sqrt{1 - \beta^2}$

(b) $t_2' - t_1' = \int_{t_1}^{t_2} dt \sqrt{1 - \beta(t)^2}$

Solution to 1-2:

Suppose the γ quantum were unstable, then a lifetime should be definable and the only invariant way to define a lifetime is to measure it in the rest system of the particle (i.e., by its proper time). Such a rest system does not exist by supposition (constancy of c). Even formally

$$\text{lifetime} = t_2' - t_1' = \underbrace{(t_2 - t_1)}_{\substack{\text{observed lifetime} \\ \text{in the lab.} = \infty}} \underbrace{\sqrt{1 - \beta^2}}_{= 0}$$

Thus $t_2' - t_1' = 0 \cdot \infty$ = undetermined. Therefore the question is senseless (for all particles with $m = 0$!).

1-3 THE LORENTZ TRANSFORMATION

We now derive the transformation formula from K to K′, where K′ moves with constant velocity v as indicated in Fig. 1-1. The invariance of Δs^2 requires ($\tau = ict$)

$$\Delta s^2 = -(\Delta x^2 + \Delta y^2 + \Delta z^2 + \Delta\tau^2)$$

$$= -(\Delta x'^2 + \Delta y'^2 + \Delta z'^2 + \Delta\tau'^2)$$

If we exclude translations in the $xyz\tau$ space, the only transformations leaving Δs^2 invariant are rotations. We are not interested in space rotations, and in fact Fig. 1-1 singles out the rotation in the $x\tau$ plane, since only x and the time are involved, y and z staying constant.

Let α be the angle of rotation. The transformation must be of the form

$$\left.\begin{aligned} x &= x' \cos\alpha - \tau' \sin\alpha \\ \tau &= x' \sin\alpha + \tau' \cos\alpha \end{aligned}\right\} \quad \begin{aligned}&(y = y' \text{ and } z = z' \\ &\text{will not be mentioned)}\end{aligned} \tag{1-8}$$

We now determine α by considering an example: We are in K and observe the origin of K′ moving with velocity v in our positive x direction. Its motion in our system is described by x and τ, in the system K′ by $x' = 0$ and τ'. Hence

$$x = -\tau' \sin\alpha \,, \qquad \tau = \tau' \cos\alpha \qquad \text{and} \qquad \frac{x}{\tau} = \frac{v}{ic} = -\tan\alpha \equiv -i\beta$$

Now †

$$\cos\alpha = \frac{1}{\sqrt{1 + \tan^2\alpha}} = \frac{1}{\sqrt{1 - \beta^2}} \equiv \gamma$$

$$\sin\alpha = \frac{\tan\alpha}{\sqrt{1 + \tan^2\alpha}} = \frac{i\beta}{\sqrt{1 - \beta^2}} = i\beta\gamma$$

† One often uses the "rapidity" r defined by $\cosh r = \delta \quad \sinh = \beta\delta$. Then $r = i\alpha$ is the angle of an imaginary rotation and therefore additive for parallel Lorentz transformations.

Hence

$$x = x'\gamma - i \cdot ict'\beta\gamma = \gamma(x' + \beta ct')$$

$$ct = -ix'i\beta\gamma - i \cdot ict'\gamma = \gamma(ct' + \beta x') \qquad (1\text{-}9)$$

Lorentz transformation

Compare Fig. 1-1, which gives the meaning of this transformation.

Problems:

1-3. Use (1-9) and the fact that any vector can be decomposed into a component in a given direction and another component perpendicular to it to establish the most general form† of the Lorentz transformation between two intertial systems K and K′, where K′ moves with

$$\beta \equiv \frac{\mathbf{v}}{c}$$

with respect to K.

1-4. Discuss this general transformation: (a) specialize it to retain (1-9); (b) solve it for the primed coordinates and verify the solution; (c) go to the nonrelativistic limit; (d) derive the Lorentz contraction and time dilatation from the general formula.

Solution to 1-3:

We decompose x into a component parallel to $\boldsymbol{\beta}$ and one perpendicular to $\boldsymbol{\beta}$:

$$\mathbf{x}' = \mathbf{x}'_{\parallel} + \mathbf{x}'_{\perp} = \underbrace{\boldsymbol{\beta}\frac{\boldsymbol{\beta}\mathbf{x}'}{\beta^2}}_{\mathbf{x}'_{\parallel}} + \underbrace{\left(\mathbf{x}' - \boldsymbol{\beta}\frac{\boldsymbol{\beta}\mathbf{x}'}{\beta^2}\right)}_{\mathbf{x}'_{\perp}}$$

To $\mathbf{x}'_{\parallel}$ we apply (1-9), whereas $\mathbf{x}'_{\perp}$ remains untransformed:

$$\mathbf{x}'_{\parallel} = \gamma(\mathbf{x}'_{\parallel} + c\boldsymbol{\beta}t')$$

$$ct = \gamma(ct' + \boldsymbol{\beta}\mathbf{x}'_{\parallel}) = \gamma(ct' + \boldsymbol{\beta}\mathbf{x}')$$

$$\mathbf{x}_{\perp} = \mathbf{x}'_{\perp}$$

†Without rotation in space.

Hence

$$\mathbf{x} = \mathbf{x}_{\parallel} + \mathbf{x}_{\perp} = \gamma\left(\boldsymbol{\beta}\,\frac{\boldsymbol{\beta}\mathbf{x}'}{\beta^2} + c\boldsymbol{\beta}t'\right) + \mathbf{x}' - \boldsymbol{\beta}\frac{\boldsymbol{\beta}\mathbf{x}'}{\beta^2}$$

$$\mathbf{x} = \mathbf{x}' + \boldsymbol{\beta}\left(\boldsymbol{\beta}\mathbf{x}'\,\frac{\gamma - 1}{\beta^2} + \gamma ct'\right)$$

Finally with

$$\beta^2 = \frac{\gamma^2 - 1}{\gamma^2}$$

$$\boxed{\begin{aligned} \mathbf{x} &= \mathbf{x}' + \boldsymbol{\beta}\gamma\left(\frac{\gamma}{\gamma + 1}\,\boldsymbol{\beta}\mathbf{x}' + ct'\right) \\ ct &= \gamma(ct' + \boldsymbol{\beta}\mathbf{x}') \end{aligned}} \qquad (1\text{-}10)$$

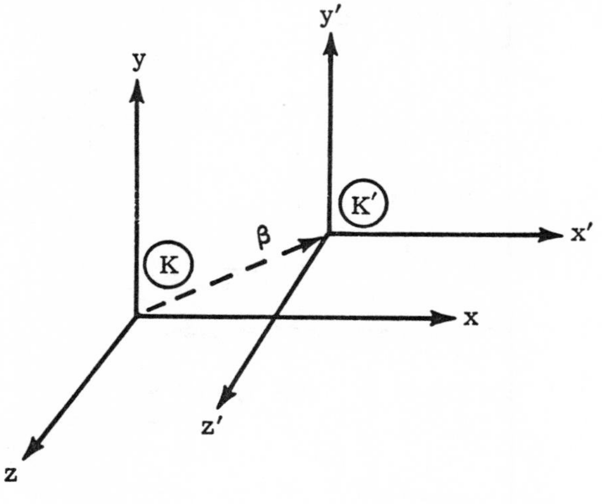

Solution to 1-4:
(a) $\boldsymbol{\beta} \parallel x$ gives

$$y = y'$$

$$z = z'$$

$$ct = \gamma(ct' + \beta x')$$

[continued on next page]

$$\mathbf{x} = \mathbf{x}' + \beta\gamma\left(\frac{\gamma}{\gamma + 1}\,\beta\mathbf{x}' + ct'\right)$$

$$\mathbf{x}'\left(1 + \frac{\beta^2\gamma^2}{\gamma + 1}\right) = \gamma\mathbf{x}' \qquad [\beta^2\gamma^2 = \gamma^2 - 1 = (\gamma + 1)(\gamma - 1)]$$

(b) The K system moves with $-\boldsymbol{\beta}$ as seen from K′. Hence we must interchange the primed coordinates with the unprimed ones and reverse the sign of β:

$$\mathbf{x}' = \mathbf{x} + \boldsymbol{\beta}\gamma\left[\frac{\gamma}{\gamma + 1}\,\boldsymbol{\beta}\mathbf{x} - ct\right]$$

$$ct' = \gamma[ct - \boldsymbol{\beta}\mathbf{x}]$$

Verification:

$$\mathbf{x}' = \mathbf{x}' + \boldsymbol{\beta}\gamma\left[\frac{\gamma}{\gamma + 1}\,\boldsymbol{\beta}\mathbf{x}' + ct'\right]$$

$$+ \boldsymbol{\beta}\gamma\left\{\frac{\gamma}{\gamma + 1}\,\boldsymbol{\beta}\left[\mathbf{x}' + \boldsymbol{\beta}\gamma\left(\frac{\gamma}{\gamma + 1}\,\boldsymbol{\beta}\mathbf{x}' + ct'\right)\right] - \gamma(ct' + \boldsymbol{\beta}\mathbf{x}')\right\}$$

After some rearrangement:

$$\mathbf{x}' = \mathbf{x}' + \boldsymbol{\beta}\mathbf{x}'\underbrace{\left[2\beta\,\frac{\gamma^2}{\gamma + 1} - \boldsymbol{\beta}\gamma^2 + \boldsymbol{\beta}\frac{\beta^2\gamma^4}{(\gamma + 1)^2}\right]}_{\parallel}$$

$$\underbrace{\boldsymbol{\beta}\gamma^2[2(\gamma + 1) - (\gamma + 1)^2 + \underbrace{\beta^2\gamma^2}_{\gamma^2 - 1}]}_{\parallel}$$

$$\cancel{2\gamma} + \cancel{2} - \cancel{\gamma^2} - \cancel{2\gamma} - \cancel{1} + \cancel{\gamma^2} - \cancel{1} = 0$$

$$\underbrace{+ ct'\left[1 + \underbrace{\frac{\beta^2\gamma^2}{\gamma + 1}}_{\gamma - 1} - \gamma\right]}_{= 0}\boldsymbol{\beta}\gamma \qquad \text{q.e.d.}$$

(c) The nonrelativistic limit is $(\gamma \to 1;\ \beta^2 \to 0)$:

$$\mathbf{x} = \mathbf{x}' + \mathbf{v}t' \qquad \mathbf{v} = \boldsymbol{\beta}c$$

$$t = t' + \frac{\mathbf{v}\mathbf{x}'}{c^2}$$

which is not yet the Galilei transformation $(t = t')$.

(d) $$d\mathbf{x} = d\mathbf{x}' + \boldsymbol{\beta}\gamma\left(\frac{\gamma}{\gamma+1}\boldsymbol{\beta}\ d\mathbf{x}' + c\ dt'\right)$$

$$c\ dt = \gamma(c\ dt' + \boldsymbol{\beta}\ d\mathbf{x}')$$

If we wish to know how in K a length element $d\mathbf{x}'$ (which is at rest in K′) appears, we must measure the position of its end points in K simultaneously; hence for this case

$$c\ dt = 0 \qquad \text{or} \qquad c\ dt' = -\boldsymbol{\beta}\ d\mathbf{x}'$$

Inserted into the first equation

$$d\mathbf{x}\Big|_{dt=0} = d\mathbf{x}' + \boldsymbol{\beta}\gamma\left(\frac{\gamma}{\gamma+1} - 1\right)\boldsymbol{\beta}\ d\mathbf{x}'$$

$$\underbrace{d\mathbf{x}\Big|_{dt=0} = d\mathbf{x}' - \boldsymbol{\beta}\frac{\gamma}{\gamma+1}(\boldsymbol{\beta}\ d\mathbf{x}')}_{\text{generalized Lorentz contraction}}$$

If $\boldsymbol{\beta} \parallel d\mathbf{x}'$ we find $dx'[1 - \beta^2\gamma/(\gamma+1)] = dx'/\gamma$.

If we wish to know how a clock at rest in the K′ system appears in the K system, we must put $d\mathbf{x}' = 0$; hence

$$d\mathbf{x} = \boldsymbol{\beta}\gamma c\ dt'$$

$$c\ dt = \gamma c\ dt' \to dt = \gamma\ dt' \qquad \text{time dilatation}$$

Introducing this in the first equation gives

$$d\mathbf{x} = \boldsymbol{\beta}c\ dt = \mathbf{v}\ dt$$

which only says that the clock moves in K with velocity $\mathbf{v}$.

1-4 THE TRANSFORMATION OF VELOCITIES

With formula (1-10) from Problem 1-3 we obtain

$$\mathbf{dx} = \mathbf{dx}' + \boldsymbol{\beta}\gamma\left(\frac{\gamma}{\gamma + 1}\,\boldsymbol{\beta}\,\mathbf{dx}' + c\,dt'\right)$$

$$c\,dt = \gamma(c\,dt' + \boldsymbol{\beta}\,\mathbf{dx}')$$

and, by dividing,

$$\frac{1}{c}\frac{\mathbf{dx}}{dt} = \frac{\mathbf{v}}{c} = \frac{\mathbf{dx}' + \boldsymbol{\beta}\gamma\left[\frac{\gamma}{\gamma + 1}(\boldsymbol{\beta}\,\mathbf{dx}) + c\,dt'\right]}{\gamma[c\,dt' + (\boldsymbol{\beta}\,\mathbf{dx}')]}$$

or

$$\boxed{\begin{aligned}\mathbf{v} &= \frac{\mathbf{v}' + \boldsymbol{\beta}\gamma\left[\frac{\gamma}{\gamma + 1}(\boldsymbol{\beta}\mathbf{v}') + c\right]}{\gamma\left[1 + \frac{(\boldsymbol{\beta}\mathbf{v}')}{c}\right]} \\ &= \frac{\mathbf{v}' + \mathbf{V}\gamma\left[\frac{\gamma}{\gamma + 1}\frac{(\mathbf{V}\mathbf{v}')}{c^2} + 1\right]}{\gamma\left[1 + \frac{(\mathbf{V}\mathbf{v}')}{c^2}\right]}\end{aligned}} \qquad (1\text{-}11)$$

where $\mathbf{v}$ is the velocity of a point (e.g., a particle) in system K (e.g., the lab. system), $\mathbf{v}'$ its velocity in K′ (e.g., the center-of-mass system of a reaction), and $\mathbf{V} = c\boldsymbol{\beta}$ is the velocity of the system K′ as seen from K (the velocity of the CM system seen from the lab. system). One sees that the velocities add in a very complicated way. Assume them to be parallel, then no change in the direction takes place and we have

$$v = \frac{v' + \frac{\beta^2\gamma}{\gamma + 1}\,v' + V\gamma}{\gamma\left(1 + \frac{Vv'}{c^2}\right)}$$

$$\frac{\beta^2\gamma^2}{\gamma + 1} = \gamma - 1$$

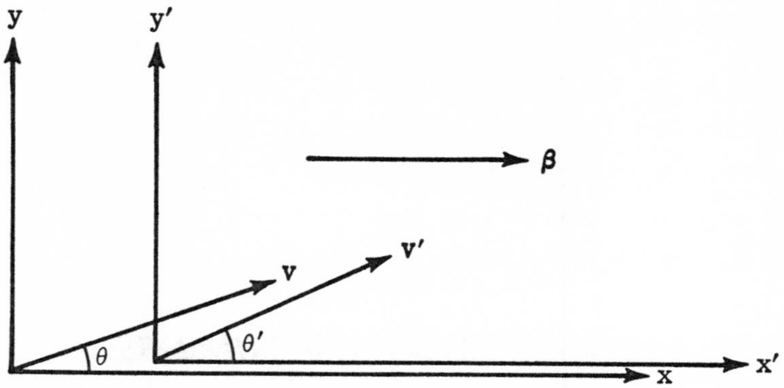

Fig. 1-3 Transformation of angles.

gives

$$v = \frac{V + v'}{1 + \dfrac{Vv'}{c^2}}$$

Thus

$$\frac{v}{c} = \frac{\dfrac{V}{c} + \dfrac{v'}{c}}{1 + \dfrac{V}{c}\dfrac{v'}{c}}$$

$v = 0$ if $V = -v'$, and $v \leq c$ always.

Choose the coordinates so that $\boldsymbol{\beta}$ points in the positive x direction and v' lies in the $x'y'$ and xy planes (see Fig. 1-3).

Then (1-11) reads

$$v_x = v\cos\theta = \frac{v'\cos\theta' + \dfrac{\beta^2\gamma^2}{\gamma + 1}v'\cos\theta' + \beta\gamma c}{\gamma\left(1 + \dfrac{\beta}{c}v'\cos\theta'\right)}$$

$$= \frac{\gamma(v'\cos\theta' + \beta c)}{\gamma\left(1 + \dfrac{\beta}{c}v'\cos\theta'\right)}$$

$$v_y = v \sin\theta = \frac{v' \sin\theta'}{\gamma\left(1 + \frac{\beta}{c} v' \cos\theta'\right)}$$

$$\boxed{\tan\theta = \frac{v' \sin\theta'}{\gamma(v' \cos\theta' + \beta c)}} \qquad (1\text{-}12)$$

which gives the transformation of the angles of a velocity.

1-5 FOUR-VECTORS AND INVARIANTS

All quantities consisting of a set of four numbers that transform under a Lorentz transformation exactly as the components of

$$ds = \{c\,dt, dx, dy, dz\}$$

according to (1-10), are called four-vectors.

We required that the Lorentz transformation should leave the line element

$$ds^2 = -dx^2 - dy^2 - dz^2 + c^2\,dt^2$$

invariant. Consequently, if four-vectors transform like ds, then the scalar product of the four-vector P with itself,

$$P \equiv \{P_t, P_x, P_y, P_z\}$$

$$P^2 \equiv -P_x^2 - P_y^2 - P_z^2 + P_t^2$$

is an invariant; then if P and Q are four-vectors,

$$(P + Q)^2 = P^2 + 2PQ + Q^2 = P'^2 + 2P'Q' + Q'^2$$

Hence

$$PQ = -p_x q_x - p_y q_y - p_z q_z + p_t q_t = \text{invariant} \qquad (1\text{-}13)$$

Some of the most important four-vectors are:

The four-dimensional radius vector:

$$X = \{ct, \mathbf{x}\}$$

The four-velocity $\left[\boldsymbol{\beta} = \frac{\mathbf{v}}{c};\ \gamma = (1 - \beta^2)^{-1/2}\right]$:

$$V = c\,\frac{dX}{ds} = \frac{dX}{d\tau} = \{c\gamma, c\gamma\boldsymbol{\beta}\} \qquad \begin{aligned} V^2 &= c^2 \text{ (timelike)} \\ \tau &= \text{proper time} \end{aligned}$$

The energy-momentum vector (four momentum):

$$P = \left\{\frac{E}{c}, \mathbf{p}\right\} = mV = c\{m\gamma, m\gamma\boldsymbol{\beta}\}; \quad P^2 = m^2c^2 \text{ (timelike)}$$

The current vector:

$$J = \{\rho c, \rho \mathbf{v}\} \qquad J^2 = \frac{\rho^2 c^2}{\gamma^2} = \rho_0^2 c^2 \text{ (timelike)}$$

(ρ_0 = density in the rest system of the volume element considered.)

1-6 TRANSFORMATIONS OF PHYSICAL QUANTITIES

Some discussion of transformation properties seems to be necessary since it is relatively easy to commit errors. The transformation properties of scalars (= invariants), vectors, tensors, etc., have their origin in the geometric nature of these objects. In addition these objects may be functions of the point to which they are attached; i.e., they may be fields.

Let us consider a constant scalar field θ (e.g., a temperature distribution). It is constant, i.e., the same throughout the whole space and therefore the same in every coordinate system.

$$\theta' = \theta$$

If we have a constant vector field $\mathbf{v}$, a rotation of the coordinate system will change the components v_i (although the object $\mathbf{v}$ itself remains the same):

$$v_i' = \alpha_{ik} v_k$$

(we always sum over double subscripts) but the scalar product of two such vectors $(\mathbf{v}\mathbf{w}) = \theta$ is invariant again:

$$v_i' w_i' = \alpha_{ik}\alpha_{ij} v_k w_j = \delta_{kj} v_k w_j = v_k w_k$$

is geometrically obvious. Similar considerations apply to a constant tensor field. Generally, we may say that for any constant field the equations

$$F' = S(T)F$$
$$x' = Tx \tag{1-14}$$

($x \equiv \{x_1, x_2, \ldots, x_n\}$ is an n-dimensional radius vector)

express that under a coordinate transformation T the constant field F transforms with a matrix S(T). The matrix S(T) may contain one single element $S(T) = 1$ if F is a scalar, four elements if F is a spinor, nine if F is a vector, etc. (These different kinds of S are called the one-, two-, three-, etc., dimensional representation of the transformation group T.) Examples worth studying are the matrices occurring in the Dirac theory. (See, e.g., J. M. Jauch and F. Rohrlich, *The Theory of Photons and Electrons*, Addison-Wesley, Reading, Mass., 1955, p. 425, or J. Schweber, *Relativistic Quantum Field Theory*, 1961, p. 70.) But in general the situation is more complicated insofar as F will be a function of the coordinates and not be constant all over the space.

As we already see in the simple case of the scalar, one cannot say that there is no change under a coordinate transformation, since

$$\theta(x) \neq \theta(x')$$

in general.

Invariance means in fact here that there is a function $\theta'(x)$ defined in such a way that

$$\theta'(x') = \theta(x)$$

It is not easy to explain the meaning of this in words because such an explanation grows so long that it makes the intuitively obvious thing unobvious. The reader is urged to make this equation clear to himself by discussing the simple example where $\theta(x)$ is, e.g., a temperature distribution in space and T a simple rotation.

We may use $x' = Tx$ or $x = T^{-1}x'$ to rewrite the equation $\theta'(x') = \theta(T^{-1}x')$, where now x' appears as variable on both sides and may be called x again. $\theta'(x) = \theta(T^{-1}x)$ is then an equivalent definition of θ'.

Thus the equation

$$\theta'(Tx) = \theta(x) \qquad \text{or} \qquad \theta'(x) = \theta(T^{-1}x)$$

expresses what is really meant if one says that $\theta(x)$ is a scalar function. We turn to the general case: let $\mathfrak{F}(P)$ be a quantity (scalar, spinor, vector, tensor) attached to the point P in our n-space. $\mathfrak{F}$ is defined as a physical quantity, not as a set of numbers [e.g., $\mathfrak{F}(P)$ may be an electric field defined in such an abstract way†: It does not refer to a particular system of coordinates but will, if coordinates are specified, have a representation (components) which depends on the system chosen. In quantum mechanics one has analogously the abstract operators and their representatives in the systems chosen—the matrices. One must clearly distinguish these two things.]

If we now introduce two different coordinate systems K and K′, we can represent $\mathfrak{F}(P)$ as functions of the coordinates x and x′, respectively,

$$P \equiv \{x_1 \cdots x_n\} \qquad \text{in } K$$

$$P \equiv \{x'_1 \cdots x'_n\} \qquad \text{in } K'$$

and

$$\mathfrak{F}(P) \equiv F(x) \qquad \text{in } K$$

$$\mathfrak{F}(P) \equiv F'(x') \qquad \text{in } K'$$

F′ will of course be different from F, if it is to describe the same physical situation at the point P.

Now we are for the moment only interested in what happens at P and we may then for a moment replace the field:

$\underline{\mathfrak{F}(P) \to \mathfrak{F}_0}$. Namely by that constant field $\mathfrak{F}_0$, which has the value $\mathfrak{F}_0 = \mathfrak{F}(P)$ everywhere. It will appear as the constant field $F(x) \equiv F_0$ in K, and as another constant field $F'(x') \equiv F'_0$ in K′. We know, however, how this constant field appears, if seen from different systems K and K′, namely,

$\underline{F'_0 = S(T)F_0}$. Where S(T) is a representation matrix of the transformation T.

This is true for a constant field $\mathfrak{F}_0$, which everywhere has the value which $\mathfrak{F}(P)$ had at the particular point P.

But in the whole argument no other point than P was used, and

---

†E.g., by an actual experimental setup (distribution of material loaded conductors in space).

we may well write the arguments x′ and x in the last equation. As far as the point P is concerned, we have

$$\mathfrak{F}(P) \equiv F(x) \qquad \text{in K}$$

$$\mathfrak{F}(P) \equiv S(T)F(x) \qquad \text{in K}'$$

but also

$$\mathfrak{F}(P) \equiv F'(x') \qquad \text{in K}'$$

and the two descriptions in K′ must be equal; hence

$$\left.\begin{aligned} &F'(x') = S(T)F(x) = S(T)F(T^{-1}x') \\ &\text{or} \\ &F(x) = S^{-1}(T)F'(x') = S^{-1}(T)F'(Tx) = S(T^{-1})F'(Tx) \end{aligned}\right\} \qquad (1\text{-}15)$$

These equations, together with

$$x' = Tx$$

give the full description of the transformation properties of the quantity F. Equations (1-15) reduce to (1-14) for a scalar or invariant function. From these considerations it should be clear that an "invariant function" is in general not a constant function.

In this discussion we choose as an example for the scalar field a temperature distribution and not a mass distribution. A mass distribution, more generally a density distribution, as such is not invariant. It becomes invariant only after multiplication with a volume element and the whole

$$dm = \rho(x_1 \cdots x_n)\ dx_1 \cdots dx_n$$

is an invariant quantity. The volume element has, however, its own particular transformation properties: It multiplies with a Jacobian determinant. We shall discuss this in Chapter 4, where the transformation of cross sections is treated. Our example of a temperature distribution avoids these additional complications.

2

CHOICE OF A SYSTEM OF UNITS

We have

$$x^2 = -x_1^2 - x_2^2 - x_3^2 + c^2t^2$$
$$P^2 = m^2c^2 \qquad (2\text{-}1)$$

In these, and in many other formulas, the velocity of light c appears explicitly. It seems therefore convenient to introduce such units that c has the numerical value 1.

On the other hand, in elementary particle physics, one has to do with quantum mechanics at the same time; the de Broglie relation between the four-momentum of a particle and its wave vector is obtained from Einstein's equation,

$$E = \hbar\omega$$

by extending it to become a relation between four-vectors:

$$P = \hbar K$$

$$P = \left\{\frac{E}{c}, p\right\} \qquad K = \left\{\frac{\omega}{c}, k\right\} \qquad (2\text{-}2)$$

by which the wave vector k is defined.

This suggests the choice of such units that Planck's constant $\hbar$ has the numerical value 1. We shall achieve both simultaneously and shall adopt from now on $\hbar = c = 1$. This does not yet fix our system of units completely. Let us briefly look into this.

We have to choose three basic units, namely, for mass, length, time. Let us choose the proton mass M to be the mass unit.

If (M), ($\hbar$), (c) denote the dimensionless numbers indicating the numerical value of these constants in a given system of units, then the elementary particle system of units is defined by

$$(M)_0 = (\hbar)_0 = (c)_0 = 1$$

The corresponding unit mass, unit length, and unit time will be denoted by m_0, ℓ_0, t_0. Then

$$M = 1 \times m_0 = (M)_{cgs} \cdot g$$

$$\hbar = 1 \times \frac{m_0 \ell_0^2}{t_0} = (\hbar)_{cgs} \cdot \frac{gcm^2}{sec}$$

$$c = 1 \times \frac{\ell_0}{t_0} = (c)_{cgs} \cdot \frac{cm}{sec}$$

We find by solving for m_0, ℓ_0, t_0:

$$m_0 = M = (M)_{cgs}\, g \qquad = \text{proton mass} = 1.672 \times 10^{-24}\ g$$

$$\ell_0 = \frac{\hbar}{MC} = \left(\frac{\hbar}{MC}\right)_{cgs} cm \qquad = \text{proton Compton wavelength} = 0.211 \times 10^{-13}\ cm$$

$$t_0 = \frac{\hbar}{MC^2} = \left(\frac{\hbar}{MC^2}\right)_{cgs} sec \qquad = \text{the time in which light travels 1 proton Compton wavelength} = 0.07 \times 10^{-23}\ sec$$

This has the consequence that now mass, length, and time are numerically measured in multiples of the proton mass.

Let μ be the mass of a particle; then

$$\mu = (\mu)M$$

The Compton wavelength of this particle is then

$$\lambda_\mu = \frac{\hbar}{\mu c} = \frac{\hbar}{(\mu)MC} = \frac{1}{\mu} \times \ell_0$$

and therefore the numerical value of the Compton wavelength becomes

$$\lambda_\mu = \frac{1}{\mu}$$

Similarly, a time is attached to it:

$$t_\mu = \frac{\hbar}{(\mu)MC^2} = \frac{1}{\mu} t_0$$

$$= \frac{1}{\mu}$$

and any given length and time can be expressed by choosing the appropriate value of μ.

Frequently this is expressed by saying: "We put $\hbar = c = 1$. Then only one dimension, namely, the mass, remains and everything is measured in terms of powers of M or M^{-1}."

This might be a matter of taste, but I personally prefer to keep all dimensions, mass, length, and time distinct, and choose the units such that the numerical values become equal to one, but not the physical quantities. In calculations, however, one practically works with equations written as if the mass were the only dimension. As mass unit one chooses the proton mass or the pion mass or, most often, the MeV or GeV.

A table of units converted from CGS to $\hbar = c = k$ (Boltzmann constant) = 1; Energy unit MeV.

$$\begin{aligned} 1\ \text{g} &= 5.612 \times 10^{26}\ \text{MeV} \\ 1\ \text{cm} &= 5.068 \times 10^{10}\ \text{MeV}^{-1} \\ 1\ \text{s} &= 1.519 \times 10^{21}\ \text{MeV}^{-1} \\ 1\ \text{MeV} &= 1.782 \times 10^{-27}\ \text{g} \\ &= 5.068 \times 10^{10}\ \text{cm}^{-1} \\ &= 1.519 \times 10^{21}\ \text{s}^{-1} \end{aligned}$$

Density	$1\ \text{cm}^{-3}$	=	7.862	$\times 10^{-33}$	MeV^3
	$1\ \text{g cm}^{-3}$	=	4.311	$\times 10^{-6}$	MeV^4
Velocity	$1\ \text{cm s}^{-1}$	=	3.336	$\times 10^{-11}$	
Acceleration	$1\ \text{cm s}^{-2}$	=	2.196	$\times 10^{-32}$	MeV
Force	1 dyn	=	1.232	$\times 10^{-5}$	MeV^2
Energy	1 erg	=	6.242	$\times 10^{5}$	MeV = 624 GeV
Temperature	1 K	=	8.616	$\times 10^{-11}$	MeV
	1 MeV	=	1.1606	$\times 10^{10}$	K

3

SOME PRACTICAL EXAMPLES FOR THE USE OF INVARIANTS

Some of the following examples are, apart from their usefulness in a high-energy laboratory, chosen to illustrate that the concept of "invariants" is not only of theoretical interest, but also leads to sometimes surprisingly easy calculations of quantities, which otherwise would be found only after lengthy algebra.

If, for example, one asks for the center-of-momentum energy of a system of particles, the straightforward, but tedious, way would be to make a Lorentz transformation of all four-momenta to the center of momentum and add all the transformed energies. Or, if one asks what is the energy of a certain particle as seen from the rest system of another one, one would transform the four-momentum of the particle in question to that system.

If one happens to know, or to have at hand, the most general form of the Lorentz transformation, namely, Eq. (1-10), these Lorentz transformations are not too difficult to carry out; we shall do this later on in an example. But this formula is not too easy to remember, and, just when one needs it, it is not available. For the above questions, and similar others, one does not need the Lorentz transformation, however. The point is this:

> if a question is of such a nature that its answer will always be the same, no matter in which Lorentz system one starts, it must be possible to formulate the answer entirely with the help of those invariants which one can build with the available four-vectors. One then finds the answer in a particular Lorentz system which one can choose freely and in such a way that the answer is there

obvious or most easy. One looks then how the invariants appear in this particular system, expresses the answer to the problem by these invariants, and one has found at the same time the general answer. This looks sometimes like hocus-pocus, as you will see in the following examples. It is worthwhile to devote some thinking to this method of calculation until one has completely understood that there is really no jugglery or guesswork in it and that it is absolutely safe.

Let us turn to the examples.

3-1 CENTER-OF-MOMENTUM (CM) ENERGY AND VELOCITY

Suppose we have in a certain Lorentz system—we call it laboratory system, but it may be any system—two particles with four-momenta p_1 and p_2 and with masses m_1 and m_2; see Fig. 3-1. (Each of the two momenta p_1 and p_2 may again stay for the total momentum of a whole system of particles.)

What is the CM energy E? This question must have an answer which is independent of the Lorentz system, in which p_1 and p_2 are given. It must be possible to give this answer in terms of the three invariants

$$p_1^2 = m_1^2 \quad \text{and} \quad p_2^2 = m_2^2$$

$$\text{and} \quad [p_1 p_2 \quad \text{or} \quad (p_1 + p_2)^2 \quad \text{or} \quad (p_1 - p_2)^2]$$

The answer is obvious in the CM system itself, namely (we denote CM quantities with an asterisk),

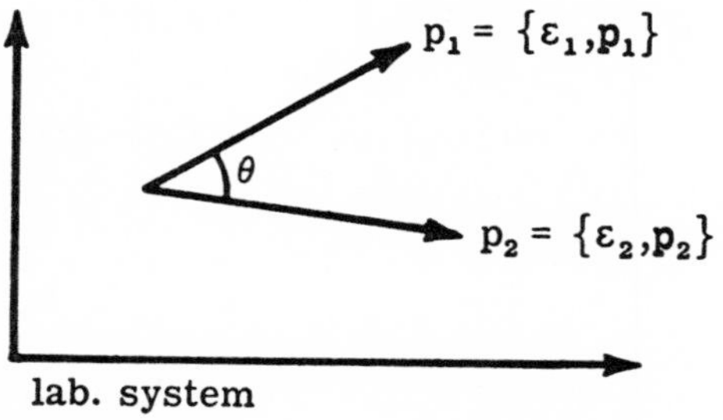

Fig. 3-1 The two-particles kinematics.

$$\mathbf{p}_1^* + \mathbf{p}_2^* = 0 \qquad \text{hence } p_1^* + p_2^* = \{\varepsilon_1^* + \varepsilon_2^*, 0\}$$

$$\text{and} \quad E^* = \varepsilon_1^* + \varepsilon_2^*$$

Hence

$$E^{*2} = (\varepsilon_1^* + \varepsilon_2^*)^2 = (p_1^* + p_2^*)^2 = (p_1 + p_2)^2$$

since $(p_1 + p_2)^2$ is invariant. We may define the total mass M of the system by the square of its total four-momentum,

$$\boxed{\begin{aligned} P^2 &= (p_1 + p_2)^2 = M^2 = E^{*2} \\ &= (\varepsilon_1 + \varepsilon_2)^2 - (\mathbf{p}_1 + \mathbf{p}_2)^2 = \text{invariant} \end{aligned}} \qquad (3\text{-}1)$$

i.e., kinematically our two particles p_1 and p_2 are equivalent to one single particle with four-momentum P and mass $M = E_{CM}$. Therefore each p_1 and p_2 can in turn be considered as representing a system of particles.

Furthermore, any four-momentum can be written

$$\mathbf{p} = m\mathbf{v}\gamma \qquad \gamma = \frac{1}{\sqrt{1 - v^2}} \qquad \varepsilon = m\gamma \qquad (3\text{-}2)$$

(This is one of the most useful formulas. It should be known by heart.)

Hence, for the total four momentum of the two-particle system

$$\mathbf{P} = M\boldsymbol{\beta}\gamma$$

$$E = M\gamma$$

Therefore

$$\beta_{CM} = \frac{\mathbf{P}}{E} = \frac{(\mathbf{p}_1 + \mathbf{p}_2)}{(\varepsilon_1 + \varepsilon_2)}$$ is the velocity of the CM seen from the lab., and

$$\gamma_{CM} = \frac{1}{\sqrt{1-\beta^2}} = \frac{E}{M} \tag{3-3}$$

$$= \frac{\varepsilon_1 + \varepsilon_2}{\sqrt{(\varepsilon_1 + \varepsilon_2)^2 - (\mathbf{p}_1 + \mathbf{p}_2)^2}}$$ is the corresponding γ

For practical calculations one has to express everything either in

$\varepsilon_1, \varepsilon_2$ and $\cos\theta$

or in

$|\mathbf{p}_1|, |\mathbf{p}_2|$ and $\cos\theta$

using

$$\varepsilon = \sqrt{m^2 + p^2}$$

Problem:

3-1. In nuclei the kinetic energy of the bound nucleons goes up to the order of 20 MeV. Illustrate formulas (3-1) and (3-2) by calculating the effect of this motion when it is parallel or antiparallel to an incoming beam of 25-GeV (kin. energy) protons (put $M \cong 1$ GeV).

(a) Which is the difference in the CM energy?

(b) Which energies must incoming protons have to produce the same CM energies on nucleons at rest?

(c) Which is the difference in the β and γ of the CM system?

Solution to 3-1:

(a) We express everything by $\varepsilon_1\varepsilon_2$ and $\cos\theta$ and obtain

$$E^{*2} = 2\varepsilon_1\varepsilon_2 + (m_1^2 + m_2^2) \mp 2\sqrt{(\varepsilon_1^2 - m_1^2)(\varepsilon_2^2 - m_2^2)}$$

where the $-$ sign is valid for parallel motion and the $+$ sign for antiparallel motion. We have then

$$m_1 = m_2 = 1$$

$$\varepsilon_1 = 1 + 0.02 \qquad \varepsilon_1^2 - 1 = 1 + 0.04 - 1 = 0.04$$

$$\varepsilon_2 = 1 + 25 \qquad \varepsilon_2^2 - 1 = 1 + 50 + 625 - 1 = 675$$

$$\sqrt{(\varepsilon_1^2 - 1)(\varepsilon_2^2 - 1)} = \sqrt{4 \times 6.75} = \sqrt{27} = 5.2$$

$$E^{*2} = 2(1 + 26.5 \pm 5.2) = \begin{cases} 65.4 & \text{antiparallel} \\ 44.6 & \text{parallel} \end{cases}$$

$$E^{*} = \begin{cases} 8.09 & \text{for antiparallel motion} \\ 7.35 & \text{for nucleon at rest} \\ 6.68 & \text{for parallel motion} \end{cases}$$

(b) If the energy of the incoming proton which produces these CM energies on a nucleon at rest is denoted by ε', then

$$E^{*2} = 2(\varepsilon' + 1) = \begin{cases} 65.4 \\ 54.0 \\ 44.6 \end{cases}$$

$$\varepsilon' = \begin{cases} 31.7 & \text{for antiparallel motion} \\ 26 & \text{for nucleon at rest} \\ 21.3 & \text{for parallel motion} \end{cases}$$

That means that the 20-MeV nucleon motion is equivalent to about 5-GeV difference in primary energy!

(c) From (3-3)

$$\beta_{\mp} = \frac{p_1 \mp p_2}{\varepsilon_1 + \varepsilon_2} = \frac{26 \mp 0.2}{27} = \begin{cases} 0.956 & \text{for antiparallel motion} \\ 0.97 & \text{for parallel motion} \end{cases}$$

$$\gamma_{\mp} = \frac{\varepsilon_1 + \varepsilon_2}{E^{(\mp)}_{cm}} = \frac{27}{\begin{Bmatrix} 8.09 \\ 6.68 \end{Bmatrix}} = \begin{cases} 3.34 & \text{for antiparallel motion} \\ 4.04 & \text{for parallel motion} \end{cases}$$

The reader should discuss the colliding-beam machine in this way!

Problem:

3-2. Suppose that a group of A nucleons (at rest) as a whole would interact with an incoming proton of 25 GeV kinetic energy.

(a) Which energy would be available for the production of particles and for kinetic energy? (put $M \cong 1$ GeV)

(b) How do β_{CM} and γ_{CM} depend on A?

Solution to 3-2:

(a) From the formula derived in problem 3-1, putting $\varepsilon_1 = m_1$, we obtain

$$E^{*2} = 2\varepsilon_1 \varepsilon_2 + m_1^2 + m_2^2$$

where

$$\varepsilon_1 = m_1 = A$$

$$\varepsilon_2 = 26$$

$$m_1 = A$$

$$m_2 = 1$$

The available energy E (nucleon conservation!) is

$$E = E^* - (A + 1) = \sqrt{52A + A^2 + 1} - (A + 1)$$

We give below a numerical example:

A	1	2	5	10	20	40	100	∞
E	5.35	7.4	10.9	13.9	16.9	19.6	22.2	25

The result for ∞ is obvious.

(b) For β we have with $\mathbf{p}_1 = 0$ and $\varepsilon_1 = A$

$$\beta(A) = \frac{26}{26 + A}$$

which as long as A remains small compared to 26, does not change very much, whereas

$$\gamma(A) = \frac{1}{\sqrt{1 - \beta^2(A)}}$$

depends on A much more critically in the neighborhood of $\beta \approx 1$.

3-2 THE ENERGY, MOMENTUM, AND VELOCITY OF ONE PARTICLE SEEN FROM THE REST SYSTEM OF ANOTHER ONE

Suppose in Fig. 3-1 we sit on particle 1, moving with it, which would be for us the energy of particle 2?

The answer to this question must always be the same, no matter in which Lorentz system we start. It must be therefore expressible by invariants and the only invariants are again

$$p_1^2 = m_1^2 \qquad p_2^2 = m_2^2$$

$$p_1 p_2 \qquad \text{or} \qquad (p_1 + p_2)^2 \qquad \text{or} \qquad (p_1 - p_2)^2$$

We call the wanted energy E_{21}. It is the energy of particle 2 if we look at it in the rest system of 1:

$$E_{21} = \varepsilon_2$$

in the system where $\mathbf{p}_1 = 0$. We only need to write this in an invariant form, namely, by expressing it by the three invariants. In this particular system the last invariant is

$$p_1 p_2 = \varepsilon_1 \varepsilon_2 = m_1 \varepsilon_2$$

Hence

$$E_{21} = \varepsilon_2 = \frac{p_1 p_2}{m_1}$$

Since the right-hand side is obviously invariant, we already have the general result. Further from

$$|\mathbf{p}_{21}|^2 = E_{21}^2 - m_2^2 = \frac{(p_1 p_2)^2 - m_1^2 m_2^2}{m_1^2}$$

and from (3-2) it follows:

> if p_1 and p_2 are the momentum four-vectors of of any two particles in any Lorentz system, then
>
> $$E_{21} = \frac{p_1 p_2}{m_1}$$
>
> $$|\mathbf{p}_{21}|^2 = \frac{(p_1 p_2)^2 - m_1^2 m_2^2}{m_1^2} \qquad (p_1 p_2 \equiv \varepsilon_1 \varepsilon_2 - \mathbf{p}_1 \mathbf{p}_2) \qquad (3\text{-}4)$$
>
> $$v_{21}^2 = \frac{|\mathbf{p}_{21}|^2}{E_{21}^2} = \frac{(p_1 p_2)^2 - m_1^2 m_2^2}{(p_1 p_2)^2}$$
>
> are the energy (E_{21}) and momentum ($|\mathbf{p}_{21}|$) of particle 2 seen from particle 1 and v_{21} is the relative velocity (symmetric in 1 and 2).

All these expressions are invariant and can be evaluated in any Lorentz system.

3-3 THE ENERGY, MOMENTUM, AND VELOCITY OF A PARTICLE SEEN FROM THE CENTER-OF-MOMENTUM SYSTEM

We solve this problem immediately by observing that we need only consider what these quantities are as seen from a fictitious particle M, namely, the "center-of-momentum-particle," whose four-momentum is

$$P = p_1 + p_2$$

and we need only apply formula (3-4) with p_1 replaced by P and p_2 by the four-momentum of that particle whose energy, momentum, and velocity we wish to know.

Let us denote center-of-momentum quantities with an asterisk; then from (3-4),

$$\begin{aligned} \varepsilon_i^* &= \frac{Pp_i}{M} \\ |\mathbf{p}_i^*|^2 &= \frac{(Pp_i)^2 - M^2 m_i^2}{M^2} \\ v_i^{*2} &= \frac{(Pp_i)^2 - M^2 m_i^2}{(Pp_i)^2} \end{aligned} \tag{3-5}$$

using explicitly

$$P = p_1 + p_2$$

and

$$\begin{aligned} p_1 p_2 &= \tfrac{1}{2}[(p_1 + p_2)^2 - p_1^2 - p_2^2] \\ &= \tfrac{1}{2}(M^2 - m_1^2 - m_2^2) \end{aligned} \tag{3-6}$$

we obtain almost immediately the following result:

$$\varepsilon_1^* = \frac{M^2 + (m_1^2 - m_2^2)}{2M}$$

$$\varepsilon_2^* = \frac{M^2 - (m_1^2 - m_2^2)}{2M}$$

$$\varepsilon_1^* + \varepsilon_2^* = M$$

$$|\mathbf{p}^*|^2 = |\mathbf{p}_1^*|^2 = |\mathbf{p}_2^*|^2 = \frac{\lambda(M^2, m_1^2, m_2^2)}{4M^2} \tag{3-7}$$

$$\lambda(a,b,c) \equiv a^2 + b^2 + c^2 - 2ab - 2bc - 2ca$$

$$= [a - (\sqrt{b} + \sqrt{c})^2][a - (\sqrt{b} - \sqrt{c})^2]$$

$$v_i^{*2} = \left(\frac{|\mathbf{p}^*|}{\varepsilon_i^*}\right)^2$$

where ε_i^* and v_i^* are energy and velocity, respectively, of particle i, as seen from their common center-of-momentum system and $M^2 = P^2 = (p_1 + p_2)^2$ is the total mass squared.

All these expressions are obviously invariant, as they answer a question which must lead to the same statement independent of the frame of reference in which p_1 and p_2 are given. Equation (3-7) gives at the same time the energies, the momentum, and the velocities of two particles m_1 and m_2 into which a particle of mass M decays.

Problem:

3-3. Given a decay process

$$M \rightarrow m_1 + m_2$$

what are the energy and momentum of particle 2 seen from particle 1?

Solution to 3-3:
We use the fact that

$$M^2 = (p_1 + p_2)^2 = m_1^2 + m_2^2 + 2p_1p_2$$

Hence

$$p_1p_2 = \tfrac{1}{2}(M^2 - m_1^2 - m_2^2)$$

This inserted into (3-4) immediately gives the answer.

4

THE LORENTZ TRANSFORMATION TO THE REST SYSTEM OF AN ARBITRARY PARTICLE

So far we only have calculated invariant quantities. This could be done without invoking the Lorentz transformation explicitly. We only made use of the invariants p_1^2, p_2^2, $(p_1 + p_2)^2$ and of the trick to calculate things in that system where the quantities had the simplest form.

If we wish to know directions of momenta, we can no longer proceed that way. But we still can immediately write down everything we wish by means of the general Lorentz transformation (1-10) (now applied to four-momenta $p \equiv \{\varepsilon, \mathbf{p}'\}$ and with $c = 1$):

$$\mathbf{p} = \mathbf{p}' + \boldsymbol{\beta}\gamma\left(\frac{\gamma}{\gamma + 1}\,\boldsymbol{\beta}\mathbf{p}' + \varepsilon'\right)$$

$$\varepsilon = \gamma(\varepsilon' + \boldsymbol{\beta}\mathbf{p}') \tag{4-1}$$

and of the relations between energy, velocity, and momentum (3-2):

$$\boldsymbol{\beta} = \frac{\mathbf{P}}{E} \qquad \gamma = \frac{E}{M} \tag{4-2}$$

which give the velocity $\boldsymbol{\beta}$ and $\gamma = 1/\sqrt{1 - \beta^2}$ for any particle (or system of particles) with (total) four-momentum $P = \{E, \mathbf{P}\}$, $P^2 = M^2$.

We solve (4-1) for quantities with a prime by interchanging them with those without a prime and changing $\boldsymbol{\beta}$ to $-\boldsymbol{\beta}$. Then the complete set of formulas is

$$\mathbf{p}' = \mathbf{p} + \boldsymbol{\beta}\gamma\left(\frac{\gamma}{\gamma+1}\boldsymbol{\beta}\mathbf{p} - \varepsilon\right) \qquad \mathbf{p} = \mathbf{p}' + \boldsymbol{\beta}\gamma\left(\frac{\gamma}{\gamma+1}\boldsymbol{\beta}\mathbf{p}' + \varepsilon'\right)$$

$$\varepsilon' = \gamma(\varepsilon - \mathbf{p}\boldsymbol{\beta}) \qquad \varepsilon = \gamma(\varepsilon' + \boldsymbol{\beta}\mathbf{p}') \qquad (4\text{-}3)$$

$$\boldsymbol{\beta} = \frac{\mathbf{P}}{E} \qquad \gamma = \frac{E}{M} \qquad P = \{E, \mathbf{P}\} \qquad P^2 = M^2$$

According to the meaning of the quantities in (4-3), these equations describe the following situation: Let P and p be the four-momenta of any two particles (or systems of particles) in a certain reference frame K. Further let K′ be the rest system of P (i.e., there $\mathbf{P}' = 0$); then (4-3) gives the transformation of the four-momentum p from K to K′ and vice versa.

Two examples:

(a) Let there be only one particle and transform to its rest system [this example is trivial and only checks Eq. (1-25)]:

$$P = p \qquad \boldsymbol{\beta} = \frac{\mathbf{p}}{\varepsilon} \qquad \gamma = \frac{\varepsilon}{m}$$

$$\mathbf{p}' = \mathbf{p} + \frac{\mathbf{p}}{m}\left[\frac{\varepsilon}{\varepsilon + m}\,\frac{\mathbf{p}^2}{\varepsilon} - \varepsilon\right] = 0$$

$$\varepsilon' = \frac{\varepsilon}{m}\left[\varepsilon - \frac{\mathbf{p}^2}{\varepsilon}\right] = m$$

as it ought to be.

(b) Let there be two particles p_1 and p_2 and put

$$P = (p_1 + p_2) = (\varepsilon_1 + \varepsilon_2, \mathbf{p}_1 + \mathbf{p}_2) \equiv (E, \mathbf{P})$$

We then obtain the transformation to the CM system (replacing the prime here by an asterisk):

$$\mathbf{p}_1^* = \mathbf{p}_1 + \frac{\mathbf{P}}{M}\left[\frac{\mathbf{P}\mathbf{p}_1}{E + M} - \varepsilon_1\right] \qquad \varepsilon_1^* = \frac{1}{M}\left[E\varepsilon_1 - \mathbf{P}\mathbf{p}_1\right] = \frac{Pp_1}{M}$$

$$\mathbf{p}_2^* = \mathbf{p}_2 + \frac{\mathbf{P}}{M}\left[\frac{\mathbf{P}\mathbf{p}_2}{E + M} - \varepsilon_2\right] \qquad \varepsilon_2^* = \frac{Pp_2}{M} \qquad \text{[compare with (3-5)!]}$$

And, as it should be

$$\mathbf{p}_1^* + \mathbf{p}_2^* = \mathbf{p}_1 + \mathbf{p}_2 + \frac{\mathbf{P}}{M}\left[\frac{\mathbf{P}(\mathbf{p}_1 + \mathbf{p}_2)}{E + M} - \varepsilon_1 - \varepsilon_2\right]$$

$$= \mathbf{P} + \frac{\mathbf{P}}{M}\left[\frac{\mathbf{P}^2}{E + M} - E\right] = 0$$

Similarly, one may transform to the rest system of particle 1 or 2 and obtain the motion of the other particle seen in that system. One may, of course, do analogous transformations if more than two particles are involved by considering groups of particles as being represented by their common four-momentum $P = p_1 + p_2 + p_3 \cdots$.

5

THE TRANSFORMATION OF DIFFERENTIAL CROSS SECTIONS; JACOBIAN DETERMINANTS

Let us discuss the following problem: Given a differential cross section in one system of coordinates, what is the corresponding differential cross section in another one?

5-1 TRANSFORMATION OF INTEGRALS

We first recall a few formulas which are derived in every book on integral calculus. If between two sets of coordinates $x_1 \cdots x_n$ and $y_1 \cdots y_n$ in an n-dimensional space a transformation

$$x_i = x_i(y_1 \cdots y_n)$$

with the inverse (5-1)

$$y_k = y_k(x_1 \cdots x_n)$$

is defined, then for integrations in this space

$$\int_{R_x} \cdots \int f(x_1 \cdots x_n)\, dx_1 \cdots dx_n$$

$$= \int_{R_y} \cdots \int f[x_1(y_1 \cdots y_n) \cdots x_n(y_1 \cdots y_n)] \times \frac{\partial(x_1 \cdots x_n)}{\partial(y_1 \cdots y_n)}\, dy_1 \cdots dy_n \qquad (5\text{-}2)$$

where R_x is a certain boundary expressed by equations in the variables $x_1 \cdots x_n$, R_y the same boundary, expressed by equations in the variables $y_1 \cdots y_n$ [one obtains it from R_x inserting $x_i = x_i(y_1 \cdots y_n)$ in it], and where

$$\frac{\partial(x_1 \cdots x_n)}{\partial(y_1 \cdots y_n)} \equiv \begin{vmatrix} \frac{\partial x_1}{\partial y_1} & \frac{\partial x_2}{\partial y_1} & \cdots & \frac{\partial x_n}{\partial y_1} \\ \vdots & & & \\ \frac{\partial x_1}{\partial y_n} & \cdots & \cdots & \frac{\partial x_n}{\partial y_n} \end{vmatrix} \tag{5-3}$$

is the "Jacobian" determinant expressing how the n-dimensional volume element $dy_1 \cdots dy_n$ differs from the element $dx_1 \cdots dx_n$.

Equation (5-2) is easy to remember: If one formally cancels

$$\frac{\partial(x_1 \cdots x_n)}{\cancel{\partial(y_1 \cdots y_n)}} \cancel{dy_1 \cdots dy_n} = dx_1 \cdots dx_n$$

and suppresses the arguments $y_1 \cdots y_n$ in f on the right-hand side, both sides are equal. If several transformations $x_i \rightarrow y_i \rightarrow z_i$ are carried out one after the other, one obtains the "chain rule":

$$\frac{\partial(x_1 \cdots x_n)}{\partial(z_1 \cdots z_n)} = \frac{\partial(x_1 \cdots x_n)}{\partial(y_1 \cdots y_n)} \frac{\partial(y_1 \cdots y_n)}{\partial(z_1 \cdots z_n)} \tag{5-4}$$

(that means: one can formally cancel), from which follows, with $z_i = x_i$ (identity)

$$\frac{\partial(x_1 \cdots x_n)}{\partial(y_1 \cdots y_n)} \frac{\partial(y_1 \cdots y_n)}{\partial(x_1 \cdots x_n)} = 1 \tag{5-5}$$

The Jacobian is 1 if and only if the volume element is preserved. Particular examples are:

The rotations and translations

The canonical transformations (see any book on classical mechanics)

Let us return again to (5-2). If we take R_x to be that volume element which in the x coordinates becomes $dx_1 \cdots dx_n$, then

R_y describes the same volume element, however, expressed in the coordinates $y_1 \cdots y_n$. We have therefore

$$f(x_1 \cdots x_n)\; dx_1 \cdots dx_n = f[x_1(y_1 \cdots y_n) \cdots] \times \frac{\partial(x_1 \cdots x_n)}{\partial(y_1 \cdots y_n)}\; dy_1 \cdots dy_n \qquad (5\text{-}6)$$

We can look at this in two different ways:

(a) Take for a moment f = const. (i.e., independent of $x_1 \cdots x_n$). Then

$$dx_1 \cdots dx_n = \frac{\partial(x_1 \cdots x_n)}{\partial(y_1 \cdots y_n)}\; dy_1 \cdots dy_n \qquad (5\text{-}7)$$

i.e., the Jacobian gives the ratio between the volume elements $dx_1 \cdots dx_n$ and $dy_1 \cdots dy_n$. So, if we consider the Jacobian as belonging to the volume element, (5-6) can be interpreted as defining a new function

$$g(y_1 \cdots y_n) \equiv f[x_1(y_1 \cdots y_n), x_2(y_1 \cdots y_n) \cdots] = f(x_1 \cdots x_n) \qquad (5\text{-}8)$$

or, since symbolically $x = T^{-1}y$ (T being the transformation),

$$g(y) = f(T^{-1}y)$$

which is the transformation law (2-2) of a scalar function (put $y = x'$ and $g = f'$ to obtain that formula). This function $g(y)$ has physically the same signification as $f(x)$, as it is related to one and the same volume element, namely, to $dx_1 \cdots dx_n$ on the left-hand side and to

$$\frac{\partial(x_1 \cdots x_n)}{\partial(y_1 \cdots y_n)}\; dy_1 \cdots dy_n$$

on the right-hand side of (5-6).

(b) For physical reasons it can be preferable not to relate the quantity on both sides to the same volume element: $dx_1 \cdots dx_n$ as well as $dy_1 \cdots dy_n$ might have convenient geometrical and/or physical interpretations and then one might relate the function to $dx_1 \cdots dx_n$ on the left-and side and to $dy_1 \cdots dy_n$ on the right-hand side. These two volume elements are frequently different not only by a numerical factor but even by their physical dimension.

If we then define a new function $h(y)$ by requiring

$$f(x_1 \cdots x_n)\ dx_1 \cdots dx_n \equiv h(y_1 \cdots y_n)\ dy_1 \cdots dy_n \tag{5-9}$$

it is clear that $f(x_1 \cdots x_n)$ and $h(y_1 \cdots y_n)$ are no longer equal. One reads off from (5-6) or finds by dividing the equation which defines $h(y)$ by $dy_1 \cdots dy_n$ [see (5-7)]:

$$h(y_1 \cdots y_n) \equiv f(x_1 \cdots x_n)\ \frac{\partial(x_1 \cdots x_n)}{\partial(y_1 \cdots y_n)} \tag{5-10}$$

(Of course, the x_i on the right-hand side are to be expressed by the y_i.)

Therefore the transformation law for scalar functions no longer applies here. Indeed, the functions $f(x_1 \cdots x_n)$, $g(y_1 \cdots y_n)$, and $h(y_1 \cdots y_n)$ have the properties of a density. But, if one transforms the coordinates in such a way that the volume element changes, the density cannot remain the same.

5-2 TRANSFORMATION OF DIFFERENTIAL CROSS SECTIONS

The practical examples which we are interested in are the transformations of cross sections and here we shall discuss two cases: the transformation to polar coordinates and the transformation from one Lorentz frame to the other.

We may define a differential cross section† either by the number of a definite kind of particles (per event) going into the volume element $dp_1\ dp_2\ dp_3$ in momentum space or by the number going into the solid-angle element and having momentum between p and $p + dp$. Call the first quantity S, then

†The quantity that we define here becomes in fact a dimensionless number after multiplication with the volume element. Therefore it is not yet a "cross section." The difference is, however, trivial in the present context, and the transformation formulas with which we end up (5-23) are correct for the numbers we define now as well as for the cross sections proper. Therefore we may use the word "cross section" throughout.

$$\frac{\partial^3 S(p_1 p_2 p_3)}{\partial p_1\, \partial p_2\, \partial p_3}\, dp_1\, dp_2\, dp_3 = \frac{\partial^3 S[p_1(p\vartheta\varphi)p_2(p\vartheta\varphi)p_3(p\vartheta\varphi)]}{\partial p_1\, \partial p_2\, \partial p_3} \times \frac{\partial(p_1 p_2 p_3)}{\partial(p\vartheta\varphi)}\, dp\, d\vartheta\, d\varphi \qquad (5\text{-}11)$$

As everybody knows

$$dp_1\, dp_2\, dp_3 = p^2 \sin\vartheta\, dp\, d\vartheta\, d\varphi$$

In other words, the Jacobian is

$$\frac{\partial(p_1 p_2 p_3)}{\partial(p\vartheta\varphi)} = p^2 \sin\vartheta \qquad (5\text{-}12)$$

One now defines, on the right-hand side of (5-11), the differential cross section with respect to momentum and solid angle, by splitting the Jacobian $p^2 \sin\vartheta$ into p^2 and $\sin\vartheta$. The first factor is absorbed into the new defined cross section, but the factor $\sin\vartheta$ remains in the differential:

$$\underbrace{\frac{\partial^3 S(p_1 p_2 p_3)}{\partial p_1\, \partial p_2\, \partial p_3} p^2}_{\dfrac{\partial^2 \sigma(p,\vartheta,\varphi)}{\partial p\, \partial\Omega}}\ \underbrace{\sin\vartheta\, dp\, d\vartheta\, d\varphi}_{dp\, d\Omega}$$

$$\left.\begin{aligned} \frac{\partial^2 \sigma(p,\vartheta,\varphi)}{\partial p\, \partial\Omega} &= p^2\, \frac{\partial^3 S(p_1, p_2, p_3)}{\partial p_1\, \partial p_2\, \partial p_3} \\ d\Omega &= \sin\vartheta\, d\vartheta\, d\varphi \end{aligned}\right\} \qquad (5\text{-}13)$$

This is an intermediate example between the two ways of looking at the transformation of a function discussed above. Here one relates the function to two different volume elements but one does not absorb the whole Jacobian into the new function. How much of it is left in the new volume element is suggested by physical considerations. The solid angle and the magnitude of the momentum are convenient; one therefore relates the cross section to them.

The next example is the transformation of a cross section from one Lorentz system K′ to another one, K. Let us choose the coordinates such that the axes of the system K′ are parallel to those of K and that their relative motion is along the z axis. The Lorentz transformation is then [see (1-9), replace x,ct by p_3,E]

$$\left.\begin{aligned} p_3 &= \gamma(p_3' + \beta E') & p_3' &= \gamma(p_3 - \beta E) \\ p_2 &= p_2' & p_2' &= p_2 \\ p_1 &= p_1' & p_1' &= p_1 \\ E &= \gamma(E' + \beta p_3') & E' &= \gamma(E - \beta p_3) \end{aligned}\right\} \tag{5-14}$$

We introduce polar coordinates

$$\begin{aligned} p_1 &= p \sin\vartheta \cos\varphi \\ p_2 &= p \sin\vartheta \sin\varphi \\ p_3 &= p \cos\vartheta \end{aligned}$$

and find that $p_2 = p_2'$ and $p_1 = p_1'$ imply $\varphi = \varphi'$. Hence

$$\left.\begin{aligned} p\cos\vartheta &= \gamma(p'\cos\vartheta' + \beta E') & p'\cos\vartheta' &= \gamma(p\cos\vartheta - \beta E) \\ p\sin\vartheta &= p'\sin\vartheta' & p'\sin\vartheta' &= p\sin\vartheta \\ \varphi &= \varphi' & \varphi' &= \varphi \\ E &= \gamma(E' + \beta p'\cos\vartheta') & E' &= \gamma(E - \beta p\cos\vartheta) \end{aligned}\right\} \tag{5-15}$$

For the transformation of the cross section we require that the number of particles going into the solid-angle element $d\Omega$ and having a momentum between p and p + dp be the same as the number going into the corresponding solid-angle element $d\Omega'$ and having a corresponding momentum between p′ and p′ + dp′:

$$\frac{\partial^2\sigma(p,\vartheta,\varphi)}{\partial p\,\partial\Omega}\,dp\,d\Omega = \frac{\partial^2\sigma'(p'\vartheta'\varphi')}{\partial p'\,\partial\Omega'}\,dp'\,d\Omega' \tag{5-16}$$

This is an example of the second way to look at a transformation, i.e., the Jacobian is absorbed into the cross section [see (5-9) and (5-10)], and consequently

$$\frac{\partial^2 \sigma(p,\vartheta,\varphi)}{\partial p\ \partial\Omega} = \frac{\partial^2 \sigma'(p'\vartheta'\varphi')}{\partial p'\ \partial\Omega'}\ \frac{\partial(p'\Omega')}{\partial(d\Omega)}$$

$$\frac{\partial^2 \sigma'(p'\vartheta'\varphi')}{\partial p'\ \partial\Omega'} = \frac{\partial^2 \sigma(p,\vartheta,\varphi)}{\partial p\ \partial\Omega}\ \frac{\partial(p\Omega)}{\partial(p'\Omega')} \tag{5-17}$$

where the primed and unprimed variables are related by (5-15). The only task which remains is to calculate

$$\frac{\partial(p\Omega)}{\partial(p'\Omega')}$$

We could do this directly, using (5-15), but we shall proceed through another way, taking advantage of the fact that for a product of transformations one obtains the product of the Jacobians [see (5-4)]. Therefore, if we transform in five steps, namely,

$$p,\Omega \rightarrow p\vartheta\varphi \rightarrow p_1p_2p_3 \rightarrow p_1'p_2'p_3' \rightarrow p'\vartheta'\varphi' \rightarrow p'\Omega'$$

The Jacobian is

$$\frac{\partial(p\Omega)}{\partial(p\vartheta\varphi)}\ \frac{\partial(p\vartheta\varphi)}{\partial(p_1p_2p_3)}\ \frac{\partial(p_1p_2p_3)}{\partial(p_1'p_2'p_3')}\ \frac{\partial(p_1'p_2'p_3')}{\partial(p'\vartheta'\varphi')}\ \frac{\partial(p'\vartheta'\varphi')}{\partial(p'\Omega')} = \frac{\partial(p\Omega)}{\partial(p'\Omega')}$$

The Lorentz transformation is contained only in the third factor. We first consider the other ones:

$$\frac{\partial(p\Omega)}{\partial(p\vartheta\varphi)} = \frac{dp\ \sin\vartheta\ d\vartheta\ d\varphi}{dp\ d\vartheta\ d\varphi} = \sin\vartheta$$

$$\frac{\partial(p\vartheta\varphi)}{\partial(p_1p_2p_3)} = \left[\frac{\partial(p_1p_2p_3)}{\partial(p\vartheta\varphi)}\right]^{-1} = \frac{1}{p^2\sin\vartheta}$$ [transformation between Cartesian and polar coordinates (5-12)]

Hence the first two and the last two factors give together simply

$$\frac{p'^2}{p^2} = \frac{\sin^2\vartheta}{\sin^2\vartheta'}$$ [see (5-15)]

Calculation of the factor in the middle remains; it can be found immediately from (5-14): since only p_3 and E are transformed, the Jacobian reduces to

$$\frac{\partial(p_1 p_2 p_3)}{\partial(p'_1 p'_2 p'_3)} = \frac{\partial p_3}{\partial p'_3} = \gamma + \beta\gamma \frac{\partial E'}{\partial p'_3} = \gamma + \beta\gamma \frac{p'_3}{E'} = \frac{E}{E'} \tag{5-18}$$

Hence, all factors together,

$$\frac{\partial(p\Omega)}{\partial(p'\Omega')} = \frac{E \sin^2 \vartheta}{E' \sin^2 \vartheta'} = \frac{p'^2 E}{p^2 E'} \tag{5-19}$$

This, introduced into (5-17), settles the question of the transformation completely.

We end this discussion by including the cases where the cross section in one or both systems is expressed in terms of solid angle and energy. For this we need three other Jacobians,

$$\frac{\partial(p\Omega)}{\partial(E'\Omega')} \qquad \frac{\partial(E\Omega)}{\partial(p'\Omega')} \qquad \frac{\partial(E\Omega)}{\partial(E'\Omega')}$$

which are found again most easily by applying the "chain rule" (5-4), and using the Jacobian (5-19), which we already know:

$$\frac{\partial(p\Omega)}{\partial(E'\Omega')} = \frac{\partial(p\Omega)}{\partial(p'\Omega')} \frac{\partial(p'\Omega')}{\partial(E'\Omega')} = \frac{\partial(p\Omega)}{\partial(p'\Omega')} \frac{E'}{p'}$$

$$= \frac{p'E}{p^2} = \frac{E}{p'} \frac{\sin^2 \vartheta}{\sin^2 \vartheta'} = \frac{E}{p} \frac{\sin \vartheta}{\sin \vartheta'} \tag{5-20}$$

from which follows immediately

$$\frac{\partial(E\Omega)}{\partial(p'\Omega')} = \frac{p'^2}{pE'} = \frac{p}{E'} \frac{\sin^2 \vartheta}{\sin^2 \vartheta'} = \frac{p'}{E'} \frac{\sin \vartheta}{\sin \vartheta'} \tag{5-21}$$

$$\frac{\partial(E\Omega)}{\partial(E'\Omega')} = \frac{\partial(E\Omega)}{\partial(p\Omega)} \frac{\partial(p\Omega)}{\partial(p'\Omega')} \frac{\partial(p'\Omega')}{\partial(E'\Omega')}$$

$$= \frac{p}{E} \frac{\partial(p\Omega)}{\partial(p'\Omega')} \frac{E'}{p'} = \frac{p'}{p} = \frac{\sin \vartheta}{\sin \vartheta'} \tag{5-22}$$

Hence, for the cross sections,

$$\left.\begin{aligned}
\frac{\partial^2\sigma(p\vartheta\varphi)}{\partial p\,\partial\Omega} &= \frac{\partial^2\sigma'(p'\vartheta'\varphi')}{\partial p'\,\partial\Omega'}\,\frac{E'\sin^2\vartheta'}{E\sin^2\vartheta}\\
\frac{\partial^2\sigma(p\vartheta\varphi)}{\partial p\,\partial\Omega} &= \frac{\partial^2\sigma'(E'\vartheta'\varphi')}{\partial E'\,\partial\Omega'}\,\frac{p}{E}\,\frac{\sin\vartheta'}{\sin\vartheta}\\
\frac{\partial^2\sigma(E\vartheta\varphi)}{\partial E\,\partial\Omega} &= \frac{\partial^2\sigma'(p'\vartheta'\varphi')}{\partial p'\,\partial\Omega'}\,\frac{E'}{p'}\,\frac{\sin\vartheta'}{\sin\vartheta}\\
\frac{\partial^2\sigma(E\vartheta\varphi)}{\partial E\,\partial\Omega} &= \frac{\partial^2\sigma'(E'\vartheta'\varphi')}{\partial E'\,\partial\Omega'}\,\frac{\sin\vartheta'}{\sin\vartheta}
\end{aligned}\right\} \tag{5-23}$$

Problem:

5-1. Prove Eq. (5-18) without explicit use of the Lorentz transformation: Define the number of particles going into the four-dimensional volume element in p space and discuss its invariance properties. Use the δ function and one integration in order to eliminate all four-momenta not belonging to the particle considered (its mass m is given).

Solution to 5-1:

Let $N(p_0 p_1 p_2 p_3)\,dp_0\,dp_1\,dp_2\,dp_3$ be the number of particles with four-momentum $p = \{p_0, \mathbf{p}\}$ going into the four-momentum element $d^4p \equiv dp_0\,dp_1\,dp_2\,dp_3$. If we then make a Lorentz transformation this number must be the same,

$$N(p)\,d^4p = N'(p')\,d^4p'$$

But as the L transformation is orthogonal, we have

$$\frac{\partial(p_0 p_1 p_2 p_3)}{\partial(p_0' p_1' p_2' p_3')} \equiv 1$$

or $d^4p = d^4p'$; hence

$$N(p) = N'(p')$$

behaves as a true scalar under L transformations (under more general transformations it behaves as a density). We now impose the condition that the particles in question have mass m by using the δ function: the equation

$$N(p)\ \delta(p^2 - m^2)\ d^4p = N'(p')\ \delta(p'^2 - m^2)\ d^4p'$$

is still obviously invariant.

We now integrate both sides from 0 to ∞ over p_0:

$$\int N(p)\ \delta(p^2 - m^2)\ dp_0\ d\mathbf{p} = \int N'(p')\ \delta(p'^2 - m^2)\ dp_0'\ d\mathbf{p}'$$

This is allowed since $p = \{p_0, \mathbf{p}\}$ is a timelike vector and no Lorentz transformation can ever change the sign of p_0. Therefore if p_0 goes from $0 \to \infty$, p_0' does the same. Now

$$\delta(f(x)) = \sum \frac{\delta(x - x_i)}{\left|\dfrac{df}{dx}\right|_{x_i}}$$

where $f(x_i) = 0$. (Proof?)

Here this gives with

$$f(p_0) = p_0^2 - \mathbf{p}^2 - m^2 \qquad p_{0,i} = \pm\sqrt{\mathbf{p}^2 + m^2} \equiv \pm E$$

$$\left|\frac{df}{dp_0}\right|_{p_{0,i}} = 2E$$

$$\boxed{\begin{aligned} \delta(p^2 - m^2) &= \frac{\delta(p_0 + E) + \delta(p_0 - E)}{2E} \\ E &= \sqrt{\mathbf{p}^2 + m^2} \end{aligned}} \qquad (5\text{-}24)$$

(A formula which one should know—at least know how to find it!)

With this in the integrals (which go over p_0, p_0' positive), we find

$$N(E,p)\ \frac{d\mathbf{p}}{E} = N'(E'p')\ \frac{d\mathbf{p}'}{E'}$$

Here, e.g., the left-hand side means the number of particles of mass m going into the momentum space element $(p_i, p_i + dp_i)$ i = 1,2,3.

But from the derivation we know that

$$N(E,\mathbf{p}) = N'(E'\mathbf{p}')$$

Hence

$$\frac{d\mathbf{p}}{E} = \frac{d\mathbf{p}'}{E'} \qquad \text{or} \qquad \frac{\partial(p_1 p_2 p_3)}{\partial(p_1' p_2' p_3')} = \frac{E}{E'} \qquad \text{q.e.d. [see (5-18)]}$$

Introducing another name for $N(E,\mathbf{p})$ we find our old formula (5-11) by putting

$$\frac{N(E,p_1 p_2 p_3)}{E} \equiv \frac{\partial^3 S(p_1 p_2 p_3)}{\partial p_1\ \partial p_2\ \partial p_3}$$

Then

$$\frac{\partial^3 S(p_1 p_2 p_3)}{\partial p_1\ \partial p_2\ \partial p_3}\ dp_1\ dp_2\ dp_3 = \frac{\partial^3 S'(p_1' p_2' p_3')}{\partial p_1'\ \partial p_2'\ \partial p_3'}\ dp_1'\ dp_2'\ dp_3'$$

5-3 CHANGE OF THE SHAPE OF A MOMENTUM SPECTRUM UNDER A LORENTZ TRANSFORMATION (QUALITATIVELY)

We now try to obtain some intuitive feeling for the transformation of a momentum spectrum by discussing the transformation from the CM to the lab. system as a function of the CM velocity (β_{CM}) in the model case where the CM spectrum consists of one single peak $p^* = p_0^*$ and is zero otherwise. The angular distribution is isotropic. (When does this model case happen?) In this discussion we shall disregard the Jacobian.

In $p^* - \vartheta^*$ polar coordinates the spectrum is $\neq 0$ only in a circular ring at $p^* = p_0^*$ (see Fig. 5-1). The particle has a velocity in the CM

$$v^* = \frac{p_0^*}{E^*} = \frac{p_0^*}{\sqrt{p_0^{*2} + m^2}}$$

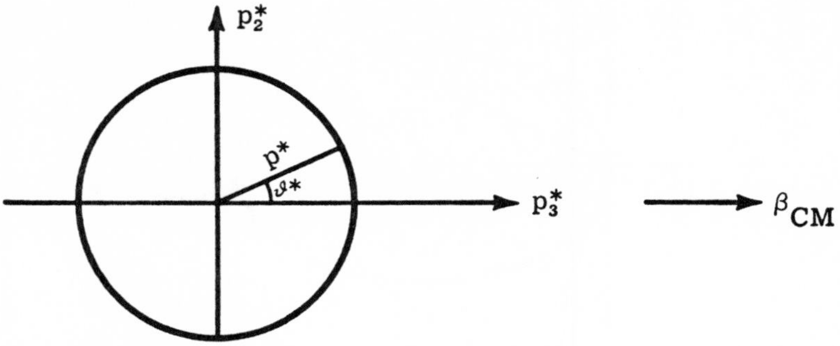

Fig. 5-1

We distinguish three cases:
(a) $\beta > v^*$
(b) $\beta = v^*$
(c) $\beta < v^*$

(a) $\beta > v^*$ (see Fig. 5-2)

All particles go more or less in the forward direction in the lab.; they all have $v_z > 0$ and $\vartheta < \pi/2$, since even those which go backward in CM are bent over by the large β. The circular ring of the $p^*\vartheta^*$ plane is shifted in the $p\vartheta$ plane so far that the origin $p = 0$ lies outside. It is no longer a circular ring (why?).

Since no particle goes backward in the lab system there must be a maximum angle $\vartheta_{max} < \pi/2$. At any given $\vartheta < \vartheta_{max}$ one observes two peaks in the lab. spectrum: one at a large momentum

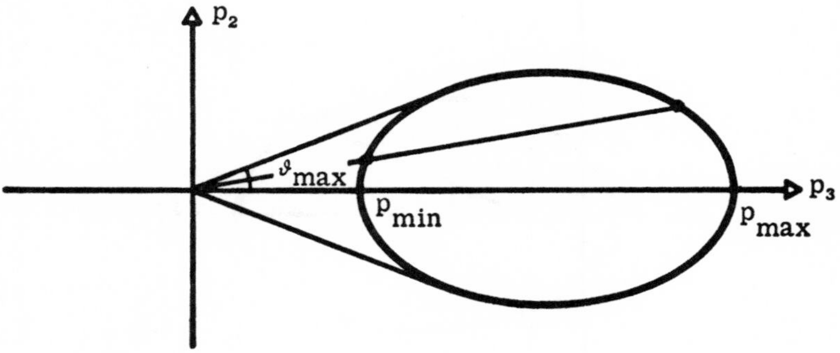

Fig. 5-2

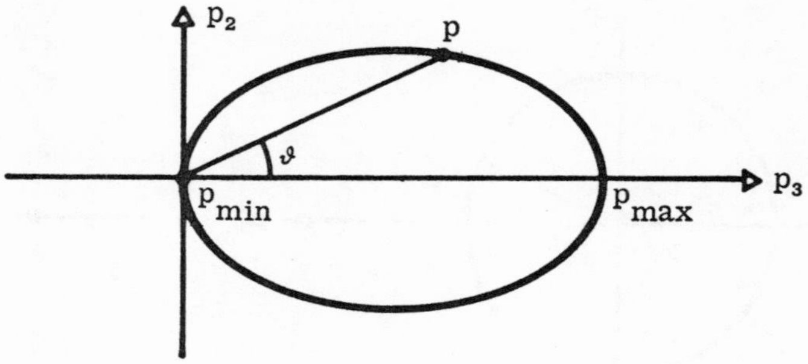

Fig. 5-3

coming from particles going forward in CM and one with a low momentum, coming from particles going backward in CM.

For $\vartheta = 0$ these two peaks have the largest separation, giving the maximal and minimal lab. momenta; for $\vartheta = \vartheta_{max}$ they coincide but they are somewhat smeared out.

(b) $\beta = v^*$ (see Fig. 5-3)

With decreasing β the maximal lab. angle increases and reaches $\pi/2$ for $\beta = v^*$; namely, when the ring reaches the origin. Hence in this case one observes still two separated peaks in the lab. for all $\vartheta < \vartheta_{max} = \pi/2$. One of them has high energy, the other one lies at $p = 0$. If $\vartheta \rightarrow \pi/2$ the high-energy peak shifts to zero, both melt together, and become smeared out.

(c) $\beta < v^*$ (see Fig. 5-4)

The ring has crossed the origin $p = 0$, which now lies inside the ring. Here also in the lab. system particles can fly backward. There

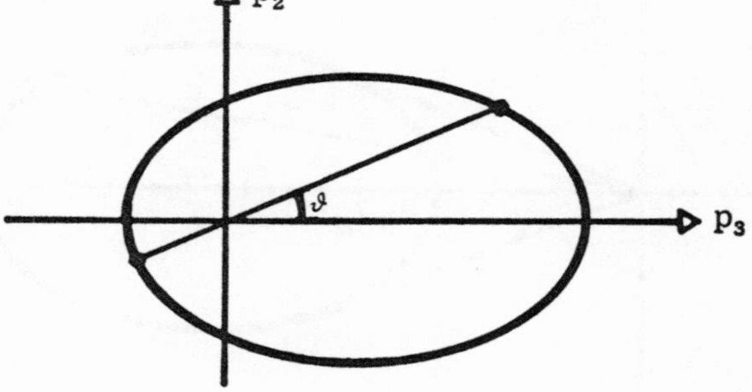

Fig. 5-4

are no longer two peaks and no maximum angle exists. This last case happens if the particles considered have zero mass since then $v = c$ is always $> \beta$. We shall discuss this in detail later.

For a general spectrum we may always imagine that it is composed of such circular δ spectra with, however, ϑ-dependent densities along the circles (CM) and with corresponding densities along the corresponding rings (lab.). The preceding considerations apply then to each of these pairs {circle (CM) ⟷ ring (lab.)}. There may, or may not, be a certain part of the CM spectrum which appears twice in the lab. system (e.g., one peak in the CM will give two peaks in the lab. if it lies in that part of the CM spectrum; it will give one peak in the lab. if it does not lie there (see Fig. 5-5).

The preceding considerations do not give the transformation of the spectra—the full story is contained in Eq. (5-21)—but they give a feeling of what happens and which part of a spectrum goes where. (What we called a "ring" is of course, in space, a "shell.")

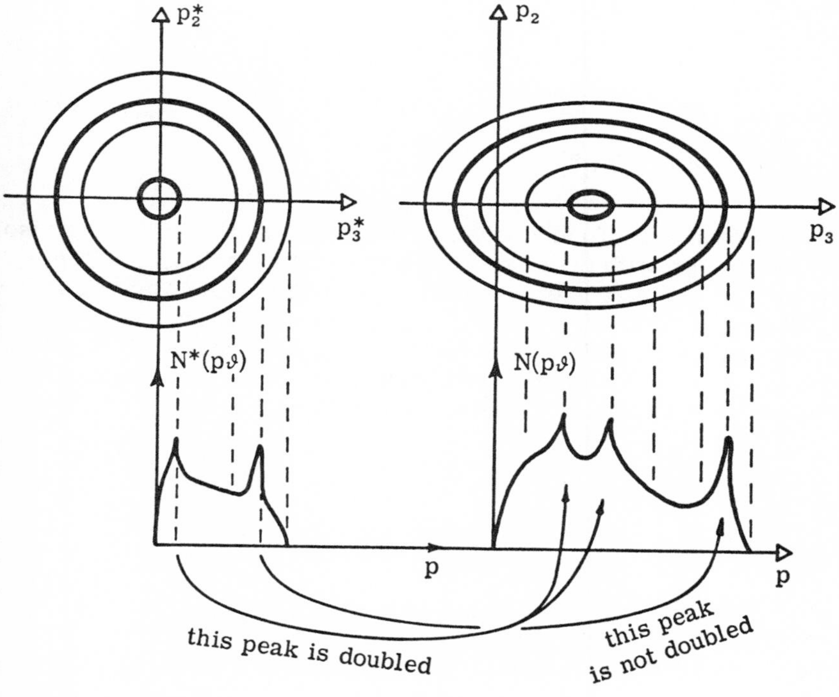

Fig. 5-5

5-4 CHANGE OF THE SHAPE OF A MOMENTUM SPECTRUM UNDER A LORENTZ TRANSFORMATION (QUANTITATIVELY)

We now carry through the preceding qualitative discussion quantitatively assuming a δ-shaped isotropic distribution in the CM (spherical shell). The following questions will be answered:

(a) Which form has the shell in the lab. system?

(b) Which are the two momenta for a given angle ϑ in the lab. system? Which is the maximum angle in the lab. system and the corresponding angle in the CM?

(c) Is there a simple graphical construction for finding the two CM momenta (directions) which will appear under the same angle in the lab. system?

We use momenta instead of velocities since the components of p transform like the space components of a four vector—which is not true for velocities. Let p* be the magnitude of the momentum in CM.

(a) The transformation for our problem is (5-14), (5-15). Only p_3 is changed. In fact,

$$p_1 = p_1^*$$

$$p_2 = p_2^* \qquad (5\text{-}25)$$

$$p_3 = \gamma[p_3^* + \beta E^*]$$

E^* is a constant. To any possible value $-p^* \leq p_3^* \leq p^*$ exists also the value $-p_3^*$ with the same p_1^* and p_2^*. If we call $\Delta p_3^* = 2\,|p_3^*|$, the corresponding length in the lab. system becomes $\Delta p_3 = \gamma \Delta p_3^*$ according to (5-25), whereas p_1^* and p_2^* remain unchanged. The spectrum, which in the CM appears to be a spherical shell with radius p^*, will appear "Lorentz-enlarged" in the lab. system, namely, as a rotational ellipsoid shell with half-axes

$$a_1 = p^*$$

$$a_2 = p^*$$

$$a_3 = \gamma p^*$$

The center of this ellipsoid (see Fig. 5-6) lies in the middle between

$$p_{3,\max} = \gamma[p^* + \beta E^*]$$

and

$$p_{3,min} = \gamma[-p^* + \beta E^*]$$

hence at

$$p_{3,center} = \gamma\beta E^*$$

Indeed, in the CM system we have $p_1^{*2} + p_2^{*2} + p_3^{*3} = p^{*2}$; hence with (5-25)

$$\frac{p_1^{*2} + p_2^{*2} + p_3^{*2}}{p^{*2}} = \frac{p_1^2}{p^{*2}} + \frac{p_2^2}{p^{*2}} + \frac{(p_3 - \beta\gamma E^*)^2}{\gamma^2 p^{*2}} = 1 \qquad (5\text{-}26)$$

which is the equation of the rotational ellipsoid in the lab. system. This ellipsoid touches the point $p_3 = 0$ if

$$p_{3,min} = \gamma[-p^* + \beta E^*] = \gamma p^*[(\beta/v^*) - 1] = 0$$

i.e., for $v^* = \beta$, as we found in the qualitative discussion. For $v^* > \beta$ it shifts over $p_3 = 0$ to the left and then the origin ($p_1 = p_2 = p_3 = 0$) remains inside.

The position of the focal points follows from $\varepsilon^2 = a_3^2 - a_2^2$:

$$\varepsilon^2 = p^{*2}(\gamma^2 - 1) = \beta^2\gamma^2 p^{*2}$$

Since ε is the distance of the focal points from the center these points lie at

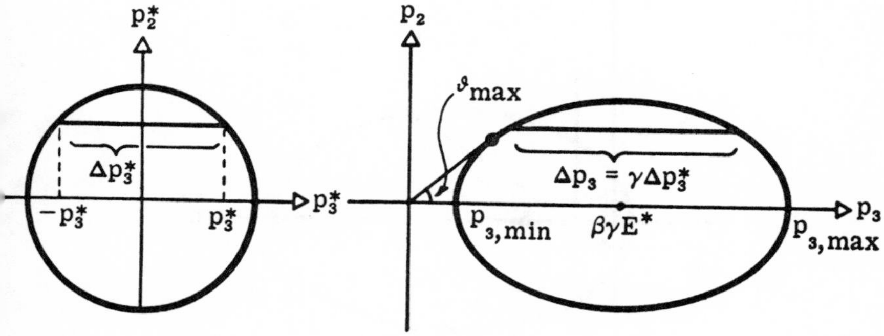

Fig. 5-6

$$f_{1,2} = \beta\gamma(E^* \pm p^*)$$

If the particles have zero mass, one focal point lies at $p_3 = 0$.

(b) We can always turn the axes such that $p_1 = 0$. Then

$$p_2 = p_3 \tan\vartheta$$

We introduce this into the equation of the ellipse ($p_1 = 0$!) and obtain

$$p_3^2 \tan^2\vartheta + \frac{(p_3 - \beta\gamma E^*)^2}{\gamma^2} = p^{*2}$$

This quadratic equation for p_3 has the two solutions

$$p_3^{(\pm)} = \frac{\beta\gamma E^* \pm \sqrt{\beta^2\gamma^2 E^{*2} - (1 + \gamma^2\tan^2\vartheta)(\beta^2\gamma^2 E^{*2} - \gamma^2 p^{*2})}}{1 + \gamma^2\tan^2\vartheta} \tag{5-27}$$

Since this equation involves only $\tan^2\vartheta$, it remains true even if the origin $p_1 = p_2 = p_3 = 0$ is inside the ellipse (see Fig. 5-7). The figure shows to what the two roots correspond in that case. The maximal angle implies that the two roots of (5-27) coincide (see Fig. 5-6). Hence the square root must vanish. This gives

$$\tan^2\vartheta_{max} = \frac{v^{*2}}{\gamma^2(\beta^2 - v^{*2})} \qquad \left(\text{with } v^* = \frac{p^*}{E^*}\right) \tag{5-28}$$

As we already know from our qualitative discussion, $\tan\vartheta_{max} = \infty$ for $v^* = \beta$. (For $v^* > \beta$ there is no real solution, the ellipsoid encloses the origin $p_1 = p_2 = p_3 = 0$.) The corresponding angle

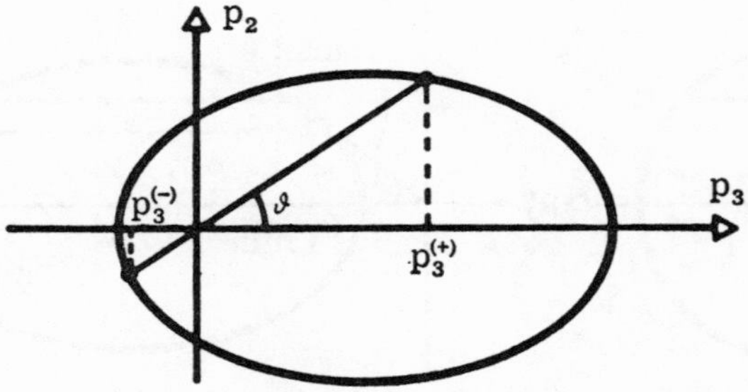

Fig. 5-7

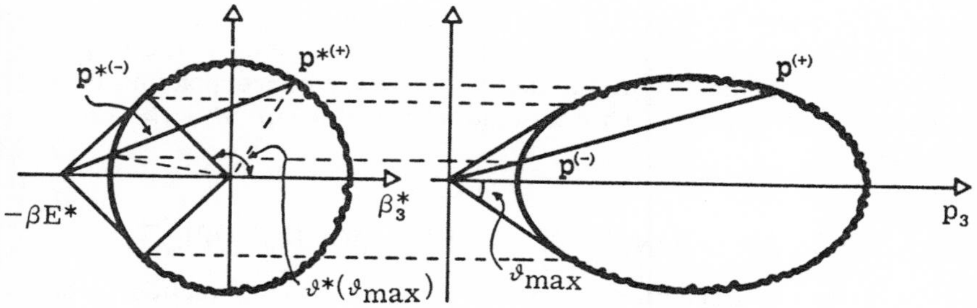

Fig. 5-8

$\vartheta^*(\vartheta_{max})$ can be found by the angle-transformation formula (1-12), but there is a simpler method.

Consider† the set of equations (5-25) and choose a direction of axes so that $p_1 = p_1^* = 0$. Then

$$p_2 = p_2^*$$

$$p_3 = \gamma [p_3^* + \beta E^*]$$

This is a mapping of the planes $(p_2 p_3)$ and $(p_2^* p_3^*)$ onto each other. The circle in the p^* plane corresponds to the ellipse in the p plane. The maximum angle ϑ_{max} in the p plane is given by the tangent from the origin to the ellipse. The corresponding angle $\vartheta^*(\vartheta_{max})$ is given by the corresponding tangent to the circle in the p^* plane. This tangent must start from that point of the p^* plane which is mapped onto the origin of the p plane, namely, from $p_2^* = 0$, $p_3^* = -\beta E^*$ (see Fig. 5-8). We read off from the figure

$$-\cos \vartheta^*(\vartheta_{max}) = \frac{p^*}{\beta E^*}$$

Hence, with $p^* = v^* E^*$, we find

$$\cos \vartheta^*(\vartheta_{max}) = -\frac{v^*}{\beta} \tag{5-29}$$

(c) This last remark leads to a very simple graphical construction (see Fig. 5-8): Draw the ellipse and the circle corresponding to lab. and CM spectra. To one angle in the lab. (straight line

---

†The material through (5-29) has been revised for the second printing, with acknowledgment to Dr. A. Werbrouck of the University of Torino, Italy, for pointing out the error in the first printing.

leaving $p_2 = p_3 = 0$) and two corresponding momenta (the intersections of the straight line with the ellipse) correspond in the CM system two angles and two momenta such that for corresponding momenta $p_2 = p_2^*$ always. This method works also for $v^* > \beta$ (see Fig. 5-7).

5-5 APPEARANCE OF A FAST-MOVING OBJECT

I wish to add here an application of the foregoing considerations which results in a surprising statement: "If an observer looks at (or photographs) a fast-moving object ($\beta \approx 1$) which approaches him under a small angle α of observation then, if $\alpha \gtrsim \sqrt{1 - \beta^2}$, he sees no longer the frontside a of that object, but he can see the backside c!" (See Fig. 5-9; the object is assumed to be a cube.)

If $\beta \approx 1$, the critical angle $\alpha_0 \approx \sqrt{1 - \beta^2}$ may be very small. If then an object appears under an angle $\alpha \geq \alpha_0$, one would see practically only the frontside a, if the object would not move; whereas our fast-moving object will show us no longer the frontside a but b and the backside c.

To prove this statement we have only to apply our above considerations to the transformation of spectra. Assume the whole surface of the cube to be covered with light sources which emit an isotropic and monochromatic radiation. Let the object be opaque, so that any radiation which has a component toward the object will be absorbed.

Now consider the radiation of one of these light points. It has all the properties we required in our model case for the discussion of how a spectrum transforms. We meet here the case in which the velocity v^* of the particles in the object's frame (CM) is greater than β. Hence the situation is as shown in Fig. 5-10. We apply our

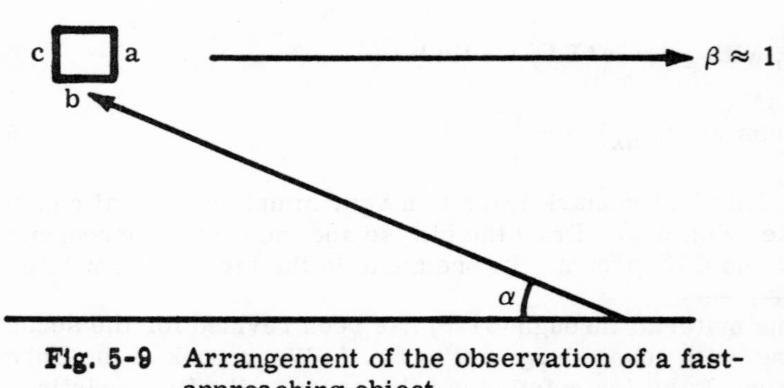

Fig. 5-9 Arrangement of the observation of a fast-approaching object.

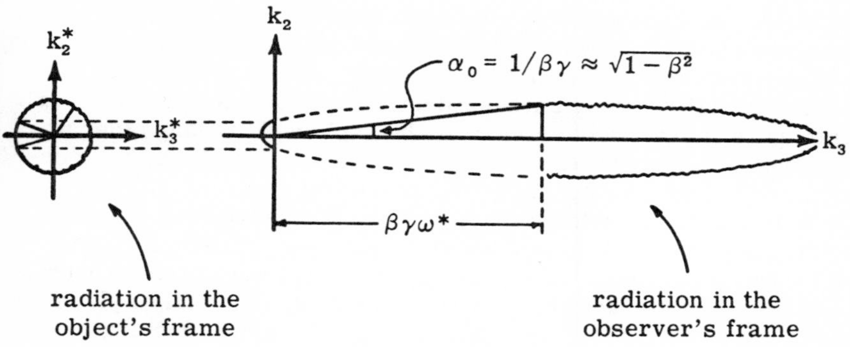

Fig. 5-10

considerations to the case $p^* = E^* = \omega^*$ (the frequency of light in the object's frame).

In the lab. system the angular and momentum distribution is then given by an ellipsoid with center at $\beta\gamma\omega^*$. Since $v^* = c = 1 > \beta$, the ellipse surrounds the origin in the lab. system. All the light in the object's frame which goes forward is emitted within the angle $\alpha_0 = 1/\beta\gamma \approx \sqrt{1-\beta^2}$, as follows immediately from Fig. 5-10 (indicated by a wavy line). A part of the light going backward in the object's frame still goes forward in the lab. system, where it appears at angles between α_0 and $\pi/2$ (indicated by broken lines). Only a small part of the light emitted backward will go backward in the lab system too (full line). Therefore the isotropic and monochromatic radiation, as it was in the rest system of the object, appears as coming from a spotlight in the lab. system: It is sharply focused in the forward direction, and, of course, its frequency depends on the angle. Therefore, if we look at the object at a certain angle (let the object be so small or so far away that α practically does not vary over the object):

We can see the radiation coming from the frontside "a" of our cube only as long as $\alpha < \alpha_0 \approx \sqrt{1-\beta^2}$.

We can see always the radiation coming from side "b."

We can even see the radiation coming from the backside "c" as soon as $\alpha > \alpha_0 \approx \sqrt{1-\beta^2}$.

To this one should add the Doppler effect, as can be seen from Fig. 5-10. What do we then observe? First, when the cube appears far away, we see its frontside "a" and, shortened by perspective, the side "b," both radiating ultraviolet. Then, if α grows, the cube seems to turn and if $\alpha = \alpha_0 = 1/\beta\gamma$, then we see only side "b," still violet. If α becomes greater than α_0, we no longer see the frontside "a," but now it has turned so far that the backside "c" becomes visible; the color becomes less violet. Finally, when $\alpha = \pi/2$, we see practically only the backside, radiating infrared. The picture remains nearly unchanged until the cube disappears ($\alpha = \pi$). This quite unexpected behavior can be explained in many other ways, and these other ways lead to a new surprise: if one looks at an object, or photographs it, this above-described apparent rotation of the object is the only thing that happens. There will be no Lorentz contraction observed: a fast-moving sphere appears as a sphere and not as a pancake. This does not mean that the Lorentz contraction did not exist; however, the Lorentz contraction takes place under the condition that the position of all points of a moving object is determined simultaneously, i.e., at one given time in the lab. system, whereas "seeing" or "photographing" supposes that the light pulses coming from a moving object do not leave it at one given time but instead arrive at the eye (or shutter) of the observer at the same time. This condition implies that they left the different points of the object at different times against the supposition under which the Lorentz contraction is derived (see p. 11). For further details see V. Weisskopf, *Phys. Today,* **13**, 9, 24 (1960).

It is left to the reader to discuss the even more curious case where we assume the object to be covered with a β-radiating material and to be photographed with a β-ray sensitive camera. To make it true science fiction assume that the β rays are monochromatic in the object's frame. Suppose then that the velocity of the object is greater than that of the electrons in the object's frame.

6

VARIABLES AND COORDINATE SYSTEMS FREQUENTLY USED IN ELASTIC SCATTERING

We shall discuss here some notations and techniques which have become usual in recent work on scattering, particularly in discussions on dispersion relations and the Mandelstam representation.

Consider an elastic scattering event and define the momenta before and after scattering, as shown in Fig. 6-1.

We use the convention that all four-momenta are ingoing. This has the advantage that one may consider any two of the four to be the incoming particles and the other two as the outgoing ones; the physical momentum of the outgoing particles is then the negative of the one we use in the present formulation. We shall, however, denote the physical momentum of an outgoing particle by a prime; if, e.g., in Fig. 6-1 the particle corresponding to the arrow with k_2 is outgoing, we call its physical momentum $k_2' = -k_2$.

6-1 THE INDEPENDENT VARIABLES OF THE SCATTERING PROCESS

We shall disregard spin, isospin, and excitation of the particles. Then the two pairs of four-momenta p_1, k_1 and p_2, k_2 completely determine the initial and final states, respectively. The transition amplitude, which describes the process quantum mechanically, can therefore depend only on these four four-vectors:

$$T_{fi} = T(p_1, k_1, p_2, k_2) \tag{6-1}$$

It seems therefore to depend on 16 variables, namely, all the components, but we shall show that these are not independent, and, therefore, the number of variables reduces to only two:

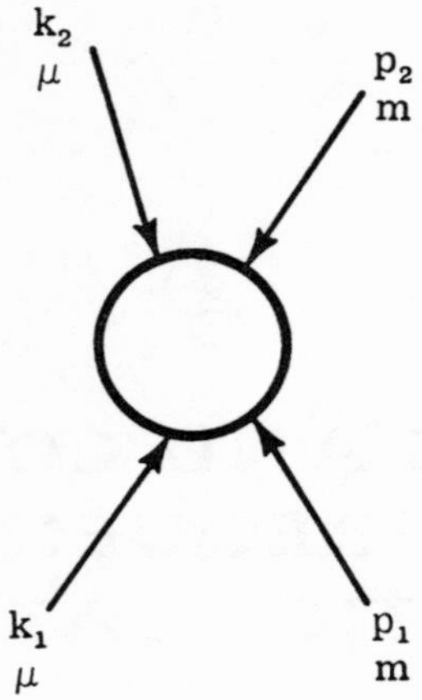

Fig. 6-1

(1) The amplitude T has to be a Lorentz invariant quantity. In fact, its square gives the probability to find a state "f" when the initial state was "i." This probability cannot depend on the Lorentz system of the observer. Therefore T must depend on the invariants which one can construct out of the involved four-momenta:

$$p_1^2,\ k_1^2,\ p_2^2,\ k_2^2,\ p_1 k_1,\ p_1 k_2,\ p_1 p_2,\ k_1 k_2,\ k_1 p_2,\ k_2 p_2$$

(2) These ten invariants are not all useful for the description:

$$p_1^2 = p_2^2 = m^2 \qquad \text{and} \qquad k_1^2 = k_2^2 = \mu^2$$

are fixed parameters which we need not mention as variables.

(3) The remaining six invariants are indeed variables which can be used to describe the scattering process. They are, however, not independent: four-momentum conservation requires

$$p_1 + k_1 + p_2 + k_2 = 0$$

This four-vector equation is equivalent to four simple equations; therefore the number of variables reduces to six minus four, namely two independent ones.

It is not arbitrary which two we select: taking, e.g.,

$$p_1 k_2 \qquad \text{and} \qquad p_2 k_1$$

we would make an impossible choice. Namely, by multiplying

$$p_1 + k_1 + p_2 + k_2 = 0 \tag{6-2}$$

by k_1, k_2, p_1, p_2, respectively, we obtain the four equations

$$\begin{aligned} k_1(p_1 + p_2) &= -\mu^2 - k_1 k_2 \\ k_2(p_1 + p_2) &= -\mu^2 - k_1 k_2 \\ p_1(k_1 + k_2) &= -m^2 - p_1 p_2 \\ p_2(k_1 + k_2) &= -m^2 - p_1 p_2 \end{aligned} \tag{6-3}$$

From the first and the second pair of equations follows

$$\begin{aligned} (k_1 - k_2)(p_1 + p_2) &= 0 \\ (p_1 - p_2)(k_1 + k_2) &= 0 \end{aligned} \tag{6-4}$$

Adding and subtracting these equations results in

$$\begin{aligned} k_1 p_1 &= k_2 p_2 \\ k_1 p_2 &= k_2 p_1 \end{aligned} \tag{6-5}$$

Thus, if we use $p_1 k_2$ as one variable, $k_1 p_2$ cannot serve as the second one since it is identical with the first one. Similarly one can use either $k_1 p_1$ or $k_2 p_2$, but not both as the variables of the process.

Adding the first pair of (6-3) one obtains

$$(k_1 + k_2)(p_1 + p_2) = -2\mu^2 - 2k_1 k_2$$

while the second pair gives

$$(p_1 + p_2)(k_1 + k_2) = -2m^2 - p_1 p_2$$

Hence

$$\begin{aligned} -\tfrac{1}{2}(k_1 + k_2)(p_1 + p_2) &= \mu^2 + k_1 k_2 = m^2 + p_1 p_2 \\ \tfrac{1}{2}(k_1 + k_2)^2 = \tfrac{1}{2}(p_1 + p_2)^2 &= \mu^2 + k_1 k_2 = m^2 + p_1 p_2 \end{aligned} \tag{6-6}$$

where $k_1 + k_2 = -(p_1 + p_2)$ has been used. If we combine this with (6-4), we see that

$$-\tfrac{1}{2}(k_1 + k_2)(p_1 + p_2) = -k_1(p_1 + p_2) = -k_2(p_1 + p_2)$$

$$= -p_1(k_1 + k_2) = -p_2(k_1 + k_2)$$

Hence

$$-k_1(p_1 + p_2) = -k_2(p_1 + p_2) = -p_1(k_1 + k_2) = -p_2(k_1 + k_2)$$

$$= \mu^2 + k_1 k_2 = m^2 + p_1 p_2 \tag{6-7}$$

Therefore $k_1 k_2$ and $p_1 p_2$ cannot serve at the same time as variables.

We can now check explicitly whether we really retain only two variables. We had six useful invariants:

$$p_1 k_1,\ p_1 k_2,\ p_1 p_2,\ k_1 k_2,\ k_1 p_2,\ k_2 p_2 \tag{6-8}$$

Assume we select the first one, then $p_2 k_2$ drops out (6-5). Take furthermore the second one, then $k_1 p_2$ drops out (6-5). We are left with

$$p_1 k_1,\ p_1 k_2 \quad \text{and} \quad p_1 p_2$$

However, from (6-7), it follows that

$$p_1 p_2 = -m^2 - p_1 k_1 - p_1 k_2$$

Therefore the variable $p_1 p_2$ is a linear combination of the first two and gives nothing new. Our particular choice leads thus to two independent variables, namely,

$$p_1 k_1 \quad \text{and} \quad p_1 k_2$$

We could of course have taken two other independent invariants; the most general choice consists of any two independent linear combinations of the six invariants (6-8).

Equations (6-3) to (6-7) are sometimes useful in calculations arising in a change of variables.

6-2 USEFUL LORENTZ SYSTEMS FOR THE DESCRIPTION OF THE SCATTERING PROCESS

Particular Lorentz systems become preferable if, by their use, convenient variables assume simple forms and/or if certain symmetries are exhibited. We therefore expect useful Lorentz systems in the cases where the three-momentum of one particle or the sum of three-momenta of two particles vanish (see Fig. 6-2).

A. $\mathbf{k}_1$ *or* $\mathbf{p}_1$ vanishes in the lab. system (if $\mathbf{k}_1$ or $\mathbf{p}_1$ refers to the target particle).

B. $\mathbf{k}_1 + \mathbf{p}_1$ *and* $\mathbf{k}_2' + \mathbf{p}_2'$ vanish in the CM system.

C. $\mathbf{k}_1 + \mathbf{k}_2'$ *or* $\mathbf{p}_1 + \mathbf{p}_2'$ vanish in the "Breit" system.

These are the most natural choices. The CM system exhibits the highest degree of symmetry. Choices in which $\mathbf{k}_1 + \mathbf{p}_2'$ or $\mathbf{p}_1 + \mathbf{k}_2'$ vanish seem not to be useful since the "k" and "p" particle will generally have different masses. If $m = \mu$, however, this reduces to case C.

Choices where the difference of two momenta vanishes, are partly impossible and partly not useful:

1. Impossible if the two momenta belong to equal masses. If, e.g., $\mathbf{k}_1 - \mathbf{k}_2' = 0$, then $|\mathbf{k}_1| = |\mathbf{k}_2'|$; hence $\omega_1 = \omega_2'$ and $(k_1 - k_2') = (\omega_1 - \omega_2', \mathbf{k}_1 - \mathbf{k}_2') = (0,0)$. In other words, if such a system exists, there is no scattering; or, if there is scattering, such a system does not exist.

2. Not useful if the two momenta belong to different masses.

When we say "not useful," we mean that hitherto such Lorentz systems have not shown practical importance. They may, perhaps, do so in particular cases. Disregarding them here, we are left essentially with the three choices: A, B, and C, mentioned above, which we shall discuss now.

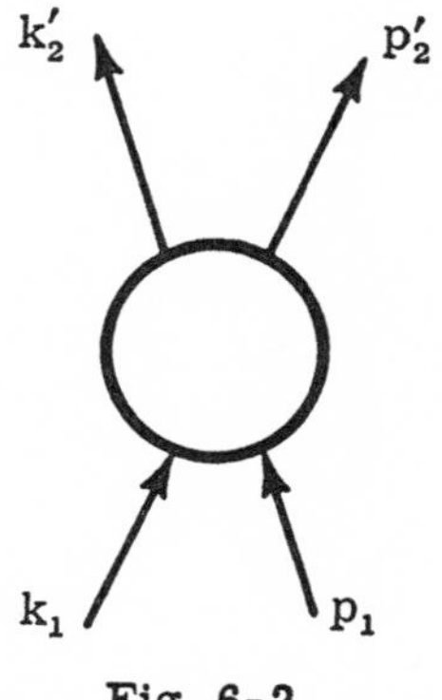

Fig. 6-2

A. The Laboratory System

This is the system where one of the incoming particles is at rest. Let this be the "p_1" particle. We then use the notation

$$p_1 = (m, 0) \qquad k_1 = (\omega_1, \mathbf{k}_1)$$

$$p_2' = (\varepsilon_2', \mathbf{p}_2') \qquad k_2' = (\omega_2', \mathbf{k}_2')$$

Useful variables are ω_1, ω_2', ε_2', and $\cos\theta_L$, where θ_L is the angle between the direction of the incoming and outgoing "k" particle. It is easy to express these variables in an invariant form using the procedure explained on p. 22. From the fact that the three-momentum $\mathbf{p}_1 = 0$, it follows at once that

$$\omega_1^{(L)} = (p_1 k_1)\frac{1}{m} = \text{lab. energy of the incoming particle}$$

$$\omega_2'^{(L)} = (p_1 k_2')\frac{1}{m} = \text{lab. energy of the scattered particle}$$

$$\varepsilon_2'^{(L)} = (p_1 p_2')\frac{1}{m} = \text{lab. energy of the target particle after the scattering} \qquad (6\text{-}9)$$

Since m is an invariant, we have already expressed these variables in an invariant form.

The scattering angle θ_L will follow from the scalar product of k_1 and k_2', namely,

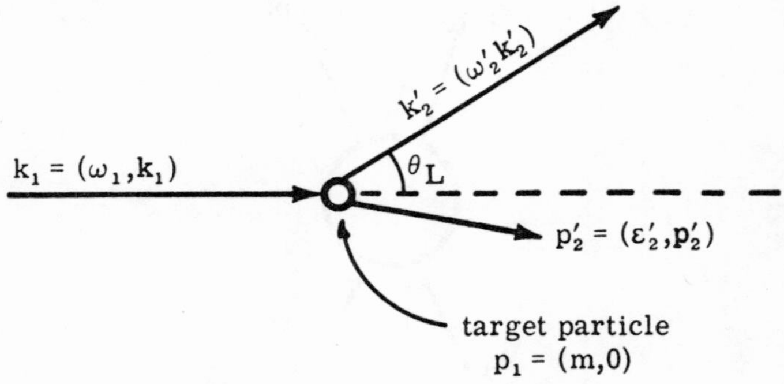

Fig. 6-3 The lab. system.

$$k_1 k_2' = \omega_1 \omega_2' - |\mathbf{k}_1|\,|\mathbf{k}_2'| \cos\theta_L$$

With $|\mathbf{k}| = \sqrt{\omega^2 - \mu^2}$ one finds

$$\cos\theta_L = \frac{\omega_1\omega_2' - k_1 k_2'}{\sqrt{(\omega_1^2 - \mu^2)(\omega_2'^2 - \mu^2)}}$$

$$= \frac{(k_1 p_1)(k_2' p_1) - m^2(k_1 k_2')}{\sqrt{[(k_1 p_1)^2 - m^2\mu^2][(k_2' p_1)^2 - m^2\mu^2]}} \qquad (6\text{-}10)$$

Here the ω's have been expressed invariantly by (6-9); this formula may be transformed into other expressions by means of Eqs. (6-3) to (6-7).

B. The Center-of-Momentum System

This system exhibits the symmetries of two-body kinematics most clearly (see Fig. 6-4). The CM system is defined by

$$\mathbf{k}_1 + \mathbf{p}_1 = \mathbf{k}_2' + \mathbf{p}_2' = 0$$

Therefore

$$|\mathbf{k}_1| = |\mathbf{p}_1| = K$$

and

$$|\mathbf{k}_2'| = |\mathbf{p}_2'| = K'$$

But K and K′ are equal for the following reason: The CM energy is given by [notation: $p \equiv (\varepsilon, \mathbf{p})$; $k \equiv (\omega, \mathbf{k})$]

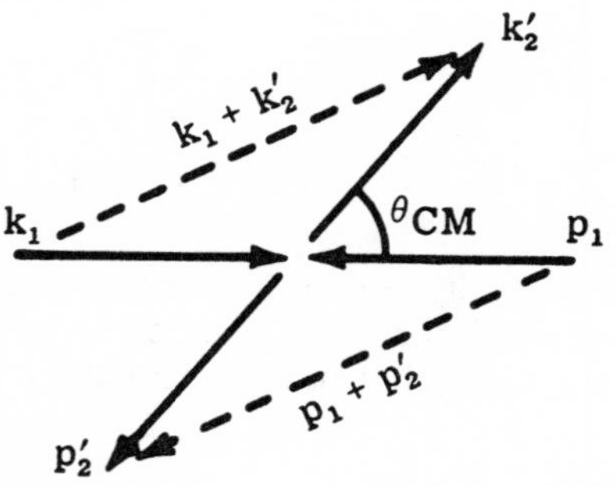

Fig. 6-4 The CM system.

$$E_{CM}^2 = (p_1 + k_1)^2 = (p_2' + k_2')^2$$

Evaluated in the CM system this becomes

$$E_{CM}^2 = (\varepsilon_1 + \omega_1)^2 = (\varepsilon_2' + \omega_2')^2$$

or

$$E_{CM}^2 = (\sqrt{K^2 + m^2} + \sqrt{K^2 + \mu^2})^2$$
$$= (\sqrt{K'^2 + m^2} + \sqrt{K'^2 + \mu^2})^2$$

hence $K = K'$. We could also have invoked our formula (3-7), which states that the momentum K is a unique function of the CM energy E_{CM} and of the masses of the particles. (There the notation is different: $K \leftrightarrow p^*$, $E_{CM} \leftrightarrow M$; $m \leftrightarrow m_1$; $\mu \leftrightarrow m_2$ are the correspondences.) (This conclusion does not hold if the outgoing particles have masses different from the incoming ones.)

From $K = K'$ follows at once

$$\begin{aligned} \varepsilon_1 &= \varepsilon_2' = \sqrt{K^2 + m^2} \\ \omega_1 &= \omega_2' = \sqrt{K^2 + \mu^2} \end{aligned} \qquad (6\text{-}11)$$

Frequently E_{CM}^2 is called s and used as a variable. The second variable cannot be K since it is uniquely related to s by means of Eq. (3-7):

$$K^2 = \frac{[s - (m + \mu)^2][s - (m - \mu)^2]}{4s}$$ = square of the CM momentum of either particle before and after scattering

$$\begin{aligned} s &= (p_1 + k_1)^2 = (p_2' + k_2')^2 = (p_1 + k_1)(p_2' + k_2') \\ &= (\sqrt{K^2 + m^2} + \sqrt{K^2 + \mu^2})^2 = (\text{CM energy})^2 \end{aligned} \qquad (6\text{-}12)$$

Either of these—but not both—may be used as variables. The scattering angle might be conveniently taken to be the second variable: It follows from $k_1 k_2'$, but more conveniently from

$$\begin{aligned} (k_1 - k_2')^2 &= 2\mu^2 - 2k_1 k_2' \\ &= 2(\mu^2 - \omega^2 + K^2 \cos \theta_{CM}) \end{aligned}$$

with

$$\omega^2 = K^2 + \mu^2$$

we have

$$t \equiv (k_1 - k_2')^2 = 2K^2(\cos\theta_{CM} - 1)$$

$$= \frac{[s - (m+\mu)^2][s - (m-\mu)^2]}{2s}(\cos\theta_{CM} - 1)$$

$$\cos\theta_{CM} = 1 + \frac{t}{2K^2} \qquad (6\text{-}13)$$

$$= 1 + \frac{2ts}{[s - (m+\mu)^2][s - (m-\mu)^2]}$$

where we introduced the frequently used notation $t = (k_1 - k_2')^2$. Note the high symmetry of the process in the CM system: all magnitudes of momenta are equal and the individual energies conserved.

C. The Breit System (Brick Wall)

This system is also useful as it exhibits symmetries. We apply such a Lorentz transformation that $\mathbf{k}_1 + \mathbf{k}_2' = 0$ (see Fig. 6-4). Therefore k_1 and k_2' will have the form

$$k_1 = (\omega, \mathbf{k})$$
$$k_2' = (\omega, -\mathbf{k}) \qquad (6\text{-}14)$$

From energy conservation it follows that the energies of the "p" particle before and after the collision, ε_1 and ε_2', must be equal; hence $|\mathbf{p}_1| = |\mathbf{p}_2'|$ and

$$p_1 = (\varepsilon, \mathbf{p}_1)$$
$$p_2' = (\varepsilon, \mathbf{p}_2') \qquad (6\text{-}15)$$

with

$$|\mathbf{p}_1| = |\mathbf{p}_2'| = p = \sqrt{\varepsilon^2 - m^2}$$

From $k_1 - k_2' = p_2' - p_1$ follows

$$k_1 - k_2' = (0, 2\mathbf{k}) = p_2' - p_1 = (0, \mathbf{p}_2' - \mathbf{p}_1) \tag{6-16}$$

2k is the "three-momentum transfer."

Equations (6-14), (6-15), and (6-16) yield the following picture. Both particles seem to be reflected on a hard wall, the "k" particle perpendicularly (see Fig. 6-5). Indeed $(\mathbf{p}_1 + \mathbf{p}_2')2\mathbf{k} = (\mathbf{p}_1 + \mathbf{p}_2') \times (\mathbf{p}_2' - \mathbf{p}_1) = \mathbf{p}^2 - \mathbf{p}^2 = 0$.

Whereas in the CM system the energies ε and ω, of the "p" and "k" particles, respectively, were not independent, they are so in the present system. Therefore they are convenient as variables. We shall express them invariantly. This is easily done by noting that

$$k_1 + k_2' = (2\omega, 0)$$

Hence

$$\omega_B^2 = \tfrac{1}{4}(k_1 + k_2')^2 \tag{6-17}$$

and

$$\varepsilon_B = \frac{1}{2}\,\frac{(p_1 + p_2')(k_1 + k_2')}{\sqrt{(k_1 + k_2')^2}} \tag{6-18}$$

In this system the variable t is very simple:

$$t = (k_1 - k_2')^2 = (0, 2\mathbf{k})^2 = -|2\mathbf{k}|^2$$

$$= \text{square of the three-momentum transfer} \tag{6-19}$$

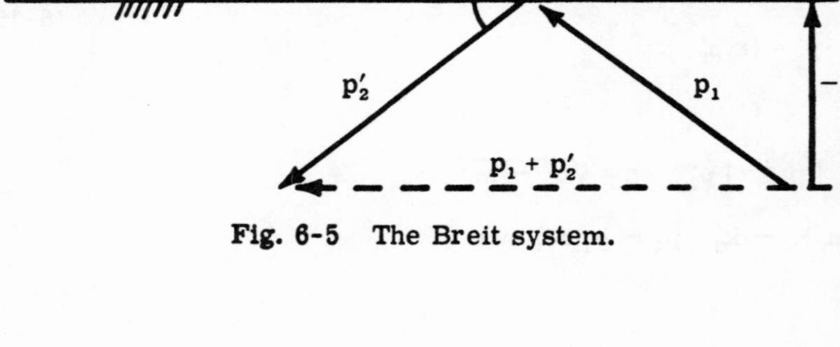

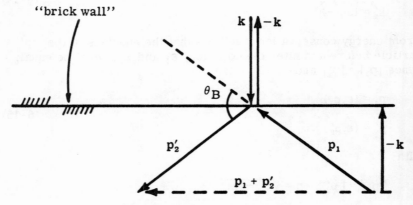

Fig. 6-5 The Breit system.

The scattering angle for the "k" particle is 180° by definition, that of the "p" particle is found from

$$(p_1 - p_2')^2 = 2p^2(\cos\theta_B - 1)$$

But

$$(p_1 - p_2')^2 = (k_1 - k_2')^2 = t$$

Hence

$$\left.\begin{aligned} \cos\theta_B &= 1 + \frac{t}{2p^2} \\ t &= (k_1 - k_2')^2 = (p_1 - p_2')^2 \\ &= 2p^2(\cos\theta_B - 1) \end{aligned}\right\} \quad \begin{aligned} p^2 &= \varepsilon^2 - m^2 \\ &[\text{see (6-18)}] \end{aligned} \tag{6-20}$$

We may express $\omega_B^2 = |\mathbf{k}|^2 + \mu^2$ by means of t:

$$\omega_B^2 = \mu^2 + \frac{t}{4} \tag{6-21}$$

6-3 THE VARIABLES s, t, u

In this section we shall use again, as in Section 6-1, the momenta p_2 and k_2, thus leaving open which particles are incoming and which are outgoing (see Fig. 6-6).

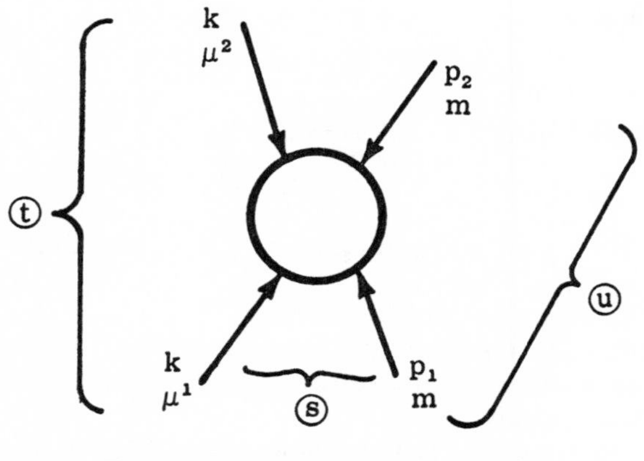

Fig. 6-6 Definition of s, t, u

In the foregoing discussion we found already that s and t were useful variables and we shall define a third one u, although all three are no longer independent of each other:

$$\begin{aligned} s &= (k_1 + p_1)^2 = (k_2 + p_2)^2 = -(k_1 + p_1)(k_2 + p_2) \\ t &= (k_1 + k_2)^2 = (p_1 + p_2)^2 = -(k_1 + k_2)(p_1 + p_2) \\ &= 2(\mu^2 + k_1 k_2) = 2(m^2 + p_1 p_2) \\ u &= (k_1 + p_2)^2 = (p_1 + k_2)^2 = -(k_1 + p_2)(p_1 + k_2) \end{aligned} \tag{6-22}$$

[see (6-6)]

The physical significance of these variables can be expressed in two ways:

(a) s is the square of the CM energy if k_1 and p_1 or k_2 and p_2 are incoming

t is the square of the CM energy if k_1 and k_2 or p_1 and p_2 are incoming

u is the square of the CM energy if k_1 and p_2 or k_2 and p_1 are incoming

This is a rather artificial description since each variable is defined by another process. The three processes in which s, t, u are the squared CM energies are called the "s, t, u channel," respectively. For example: Let $k_{1,2}$ describe pions, $p_{1,2}$ nucleons. Then the

s channel means $\pi + N \to \pi + N$

or $\pi + \overline{N} \to \pi + \overline{N}$

t channel means $\pi + \pi \to N + \overline{N}$

or $N + \overline{N} \to \pi + \pi$

u channel means $\pi + N \to \pi + N$

or $\pi + \overline{N} \to \pi + \overline{N}$

(b) If we describe the meaning of s, t, u in a definite process, e.g., the "s channel," then

s is the square of the CM energy

t is the squared four-momentum transfer. In particular it reduces to the squared three-momentum transfer in the Breit system (6-19)

u has no simple physical meaning since there is no Lorentz system where it reduces to anything obvious. This is a consequence of being the difference of physical momenta of particles with different masses (see remark on p. 61)

As s, t, u are not independent, we can write down a relation. From (6-22)

$$s + t + u = 4\mu^2 + 2m^2 + 2k_1(\underbrace{p_1 + p_2 + k_2}_{= -k_1}) = 2\mu^2 + 2m^2$$

$$s + t + u = 2\mu^2 + 2m^2 \qquad (6\text{-}23)$$

Let us anticipate the notion of the scattering amplitude, namely, that complex function which completely describes the scattering process. It will be a function of two independent invariants, but we may write it as a function of s, t, u if we only keep in mind that one of these variables is redundant. Let then

$$T(s,t,u) = \text{scattering amplitude} \qquad (6\text{-}24)$$

One can prove—independently of perturbation theory—that this function is an analytic function of any two of the variables if these are considered to be complex.

There are then certain domains in the complex st (or su or tu) space in which these variables become real and have "physical" values. These regions, as we shall see, are disconnected and belong to different physical processes, namely, e.g., the three processes described on p. 68. That T(s,t,u) is an analytic function of any two complex variables out of s, t, u means then that the "physical scattering amplitude" is the boundary value of that general function when s, t, u take on physical values. In other words, the "physical scattering amplitude" is obtained in any channel from the general function simply by specializing to the "physical values" of s, t, u for that channel. As the analytic functions are essentially determined by their singularities, it is important to know the singularities of T(stu). We are far from knowing their structure. In recent work on strong interactions, a conjecture of Mandelstam about these singularities has been widely applied. Although it has led to very intuitive descriptions of strong interaction processes and has supplied us with a new technique, it remains a conjecture. This does not exclude its value in practical limited calculations. Namely, it may turn out one day, when we know more about these things, that Mandelstam's ansatz neglected singularities which in many calculations show only little influence.

6-4 GRAPHICAL REPRESENTATION OF s, t, u; PHYSICAL REGIONS

We shall not go into the "analytic structure of scattering amplitudes" (which would require a special lecture), but only explain the graphical representation of the variables s, t, u and exhibit their "physical regions."

We remember from elementary geometry a theorem on triangles (Fig. 6-7). If from any point P the three distances g_a, g_b, g_c to the sides a, b, c, respectively, are taken, then

$$ag_a + bg_b + cg_c = ah_a = bh_b = ch_c = 2F$$

namely, two times the surface of the triangle. (This is also true for points outside the triangle if proper care of the sign of the distances g_i is taken.) Here h_a, h_b, h_c are the three heights perpendicular on a, b, c, respectively. Taking ch_c and dividing by c we have

$$\frac{a}{c} g_a + \frac{b}{c} g_b + g_c = h_c$$

With this we compare (6-23)

$$u + s + t = 2m^2 + 2\mu^2$$

and see that we only need to identify

$$\frac{a}{c} g_a = u \qquad \frac{b}{c} g_b = s \qquad g_c = t \qquad h_c = 2m^2 + 2\mu^2$$

to have our relation between s, t, u fulfilled. Therefore any three coordinate axes intersecting such that they form a triangle with

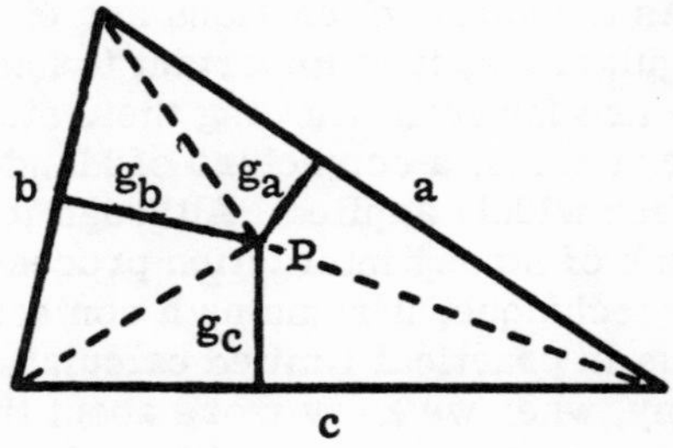

Fig. 6-7

$h_c = 2m^2 + 2\mu^2$ can serve to represent s, t, u in a plane. Of course one chooses particular triangles where the representation becomes simple.

The best choice seems to be $a = b = c$; $h = 2m^2 + 2\mu^2$ (Fig. 6-8). This is very symmetrical but has one disadvantage: The boundaries of the "physical regions" will be given in the form of equations between s and t. Such curves are easier to draw in rectangular coordinate system.

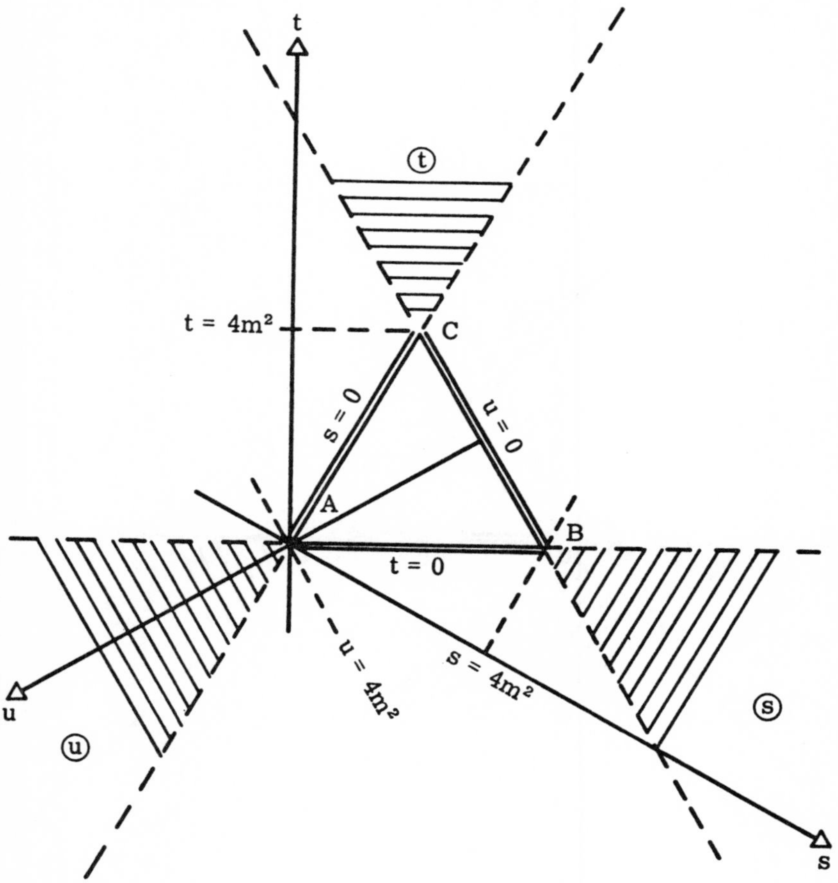

Fig. 6-8 Physical regions of s, t, u channels in symmetrical representation for $m = \mu$. Every point in the plane satisfies $s + t + u = 4m^2$.

In the latter case we choose

$$b = c = \frac{a}{\sqrt{2}} = h = 2m^2 + 2\mu^2 \qquad \text{(Fig. 6-9)}$$

Let us find the "physical regions" of s, t, u in the three possible channels. We draw first three figures (Fig. 6-10a–c). We see immediately that even for $m \neq \mu$ there is one symmetry: namely, that t is the momentum transfer in both—the s channel and the u channel—whereas s and u are interchanged; we expect therefore that the physical regions in the s and u channels

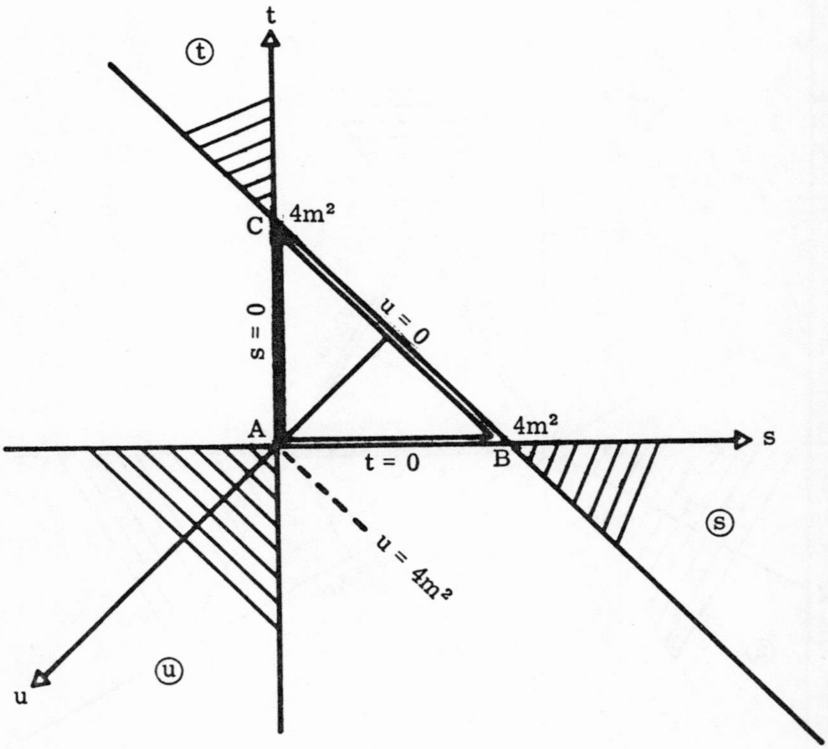

Fig. 6-9 Physical regions of s, t, u channels in Cartesian st plane for $m = \mu$. Every point in the plane satisfies $s + t + u = 4m^2$. (Note that the unit along the u axis is smaller by a factor $1/\sqrt{2}$ as compared to the s and t axes.)

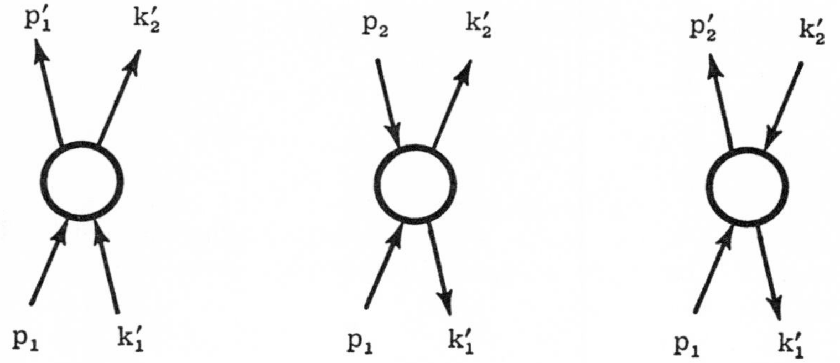

(a) s channel (b) t channel (c) u channel

Fig. 6-10

map on each other if s and u are interchanged (this is the famous *crossing symmetry*); it will show up most clearly in the symmetrical representation (Fig. 6-8, see also Fig. 6-11).

If the masses are equal, $m = \mu$, then there is more symmetry:

going from the s channel to the t channel, u keeps its meaning
going from the s channel to the u channel, t keeps its meaning
going from the t channel to the u channel, s keeps its meaning

The physical regions are therefore mapped on each other if we:
(a) interchange $s \leftrightarrow t$ and keep u
(b) interchange $s \leftrightarrow u$ and keep t
(c) interchange $t \leftrightarrow u$ and keep s

These are, in the symmetrical representation (Fig. 6-8), the reflections of the whole plane with respect to the three symmetry axes of the basic triangle ABC. In Fig. 6-9 the different scale along the axes makes the figure apparently less symmetric, but one easily translates the physical regions from Fig. 6-8 to Fig. 6-9.

This symmetry allows us to discuss the s channel only. We shall restrict the consideration to the most symmetric case $m = \mu$. We have in the s channel (CM system)

$$s = (p_1 + k_1)^2 = (p_2' + k_2')^2 = (2E)^2 = 4(m^2 + K^2)$$

$$t = (p_2' - p_1)^2 = (k_2' - k_1)^2 = 2K^2(\cos \theta_{CM} - 1)$$

with K the momentum of all four particles. Hence the "physical region" in the s channel is given by

$$4m^2 \leq s$$

$$t_{min} \leq t \leq 0$$

$$t_{min} = -4K^2 = 4m^2 - s$$

With $s + t + u = 4m^2$ we find $s + t_{min} + u = 4m^2 = s + t_{min}$. Hence the boundary $t_{min} = 4m^2 - s$ is identical with the line $u = 0$. The physical region of the s channel is therefore given by the two conditions

$$t \leq 0$$

$$u \leq 0$$

This region is shown in Figs. 6-8 and 6-9 shaded and marked Ⓢ. The corresponding regions for the other two channels follow from the above symmetry considerations. The case $m > \mu$ will be treated in Problem 6-1.

Only in the physical regions can physical measurements yield information about the scattering amplitude. A remarkable circumstance is that the different channels correspond to very different processes: assume that p and k mean nucleon and pion, respectively. Then

s channel: $\pi - N$ scattering (elastic)
t channel: $N + \overline{N} \rightarrow 2\pi$ (or $\pi + \pi \rightarrow N + \overline{N}$)
u channel: $\pi - N$ scattering (crossed process with respect to s channel)

All these processes, different as they are, become "one and the same" if one considers the whole complex stu plane.

Problem:

6-1. Discuss the physical regions in the s, t, u channels, respectively, in the CM system if $m > \mu$.

Solution to 6-1:

We consider first the s channel. In the general case with two different masses we have

$$s = (k_1 + p_1)^2 = (k_2' + p_2')^2 = m^2 + \mu^2 + 2\varepsilon\omega + 2K^2 \geq (m + \mu)^2$$

$$t = (p_2' - p_1)^2 = (k_2' - k_1)^2 = 2K^2(\cos\theta - 1)$$

We note first that, whatever t means, the cos θ has a physical meaning in all three channels, whereas K^2 might become negative (i.e., t positive, namely, in the t channel). If we therefore express K^2, which is an invariant in the sense of p. 22, as a function of s, we can immediately obtain a relation between s and t which determines the boundary of the physical region. Now K is the magnitude of the momentum of all four particles, and this is a unique function of the CM energy and the masses of the particles involved. We have derived a formula for this, namely, (3-7). We must replace M^2 by s, m_1 by m, m_2 by μ, and $|p^*|^2$ by K^2:

$$K^2 = \frac{[s - (m + \mu)^2][s - (m - \mu)^2]}{4s}$$

Therefore we obtain

$$t = \frac{[s - (m + \mu)^2][s - (m - \mu)^2]}{2s} (\cos\theta - 1) \qquad (6\text{-}25)$$

$$\left.\begin{array}{l} t_{max} = 0, \text{ namely, for } \cos\theta = 1 \text{ is one boundary} \\ \text{The other one is then} \\ t_{min} = -\dfrac{[s - (m + \mu)^2][s - (m - \mu)^2]}{s} \end{array}\right\} \qquad (6\text{-}26)$$

This boundary is a hyperbola. We find its asymptotes by letting

(a) $s \to +0 \qquad t \to -\infty$

(b) $s \to +\infty \qquad t \to -\infty \qquad$ as $\qquad t \to -s + 2(m^2 + \mu^2)$

The first one is the line $s = 0$, the second one is the line $u = 0$ (since $u = 2m^2 + 2\mu^2 - s - t$). The hyperbola intersects the line $t = 0$ at $s = (m \pm \mu)^2$, as Eq. (6-26) shows. We draw this hyperbola in our symmetrical representation (Fig. 6-11). Then Eq. (6-26) determines the shaded region marked ⓢ as the physical region of the s channel. The physical region for the u channel follows immediately from crossing symmetry (see remarks on p. 73): shaded region marked ⓤ. It remains now to find the physical region for the t channel.

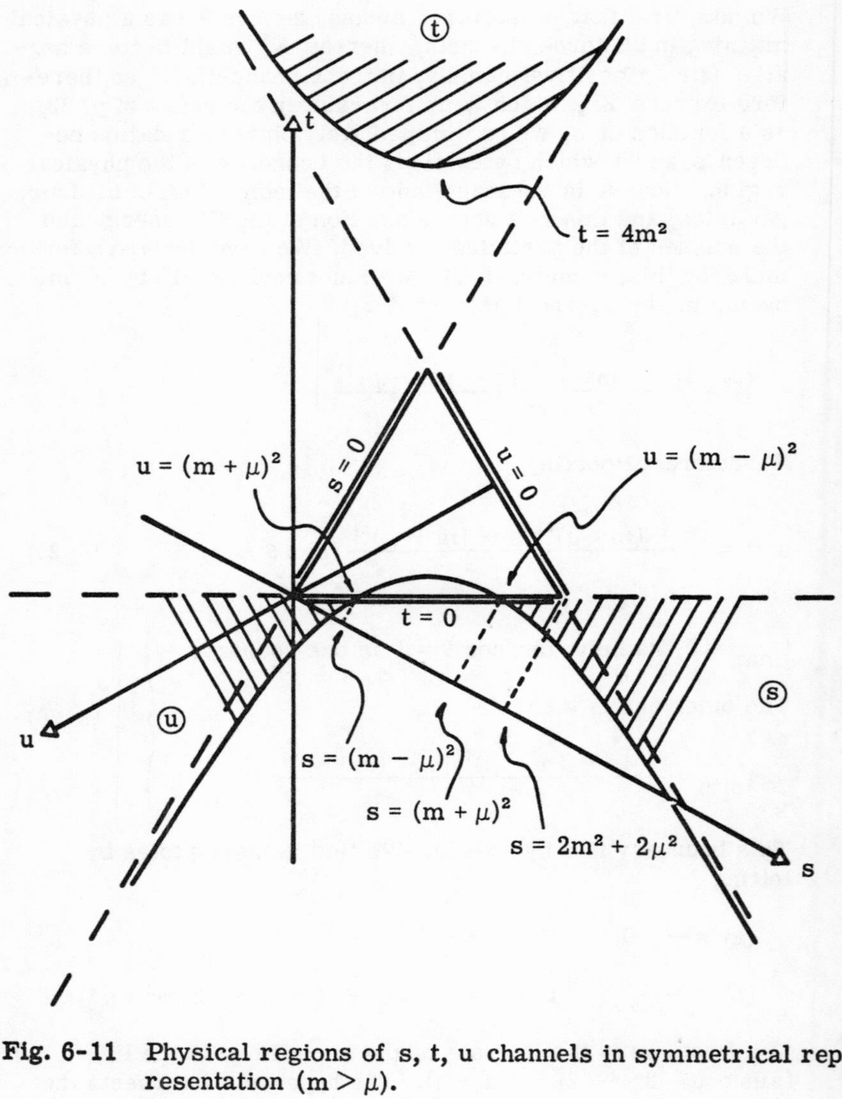

Fig. 6-11 Physical regions of s, t, u channels in symmetrical representation ($m > \mu$).

Obviously, $t = (p_1 + p_2)^2$ implies

$$t \geq 4m^2$$

Here the two incoming particles have both mass m and

therefore equal energies E. But this is also the energy of the outgoing particles

$$t = (p_1 + p_2)^2 = 4E^2 = (k_1' + k_2')^2$$

The momentum transfer, $s = (p_1 - k_1')^2$, is here between particles of different mass. Therefore

$$s = m^2 + \mu^2 - 2E + 2\sqrt{(E^2 - m^2)(E^2 - \mu^2)}\ \cos\varphi$$

$$= -(p_1 - k_1')^2 < 0$$

where φ is the angle between p_1 and k_1'. Putting $\cos\varphi = \pm 1$ we obtain the extreme s values (still < 0),

$$s_{extr} = -4E^2 + 2(m^2 + \mu^2) - \frac{(\mu^2 - m^2)^2}{s_{extr}}$$

But $4E^2 = t$, hence

$$t = -s_{extr} + 2(m^2 + \mu^2) - \frac{(\mu^2 - m^2)^2}{s_{extr}} \qquad t \geq 4m^2 \qquad (6\text{-}27)$$

This, in fact, is the same as Eq. (6-26) for t_{min}. Here, however, it determines the s_{extr} for given $t \geq 4m^2$. Obviously this is the other branch of the hyperbola. From this follows then the physical region in the t channel. Figures 6-11 and 6-12 show the physical regions shaded and marked with ⓢ ⓣ ⓤ, respectively.

We could have argued immediately: Equation (6-25) gives a relation between s and t and $\cos\theta$. As in all channels $\cos\theta$ has a physical significance, it is always bound between ±1. One value, $\cos\theta = +1$, leads to $t = 0$ as a boundary. The other one gives the full hyperbola

$$t = -s + 2(m^2 + \mu^2) - \frac{(\mu^2 - m^2)^2}{s}$$

as another boundary. The two branches belong to two situations:

(a) $t < 0$; s (or u) channel. Then the lower branch is selected and it determines t_{min}.

(b) $t > 0$; this is the t channel. The upper branch is selected and determines the extreme values of s.

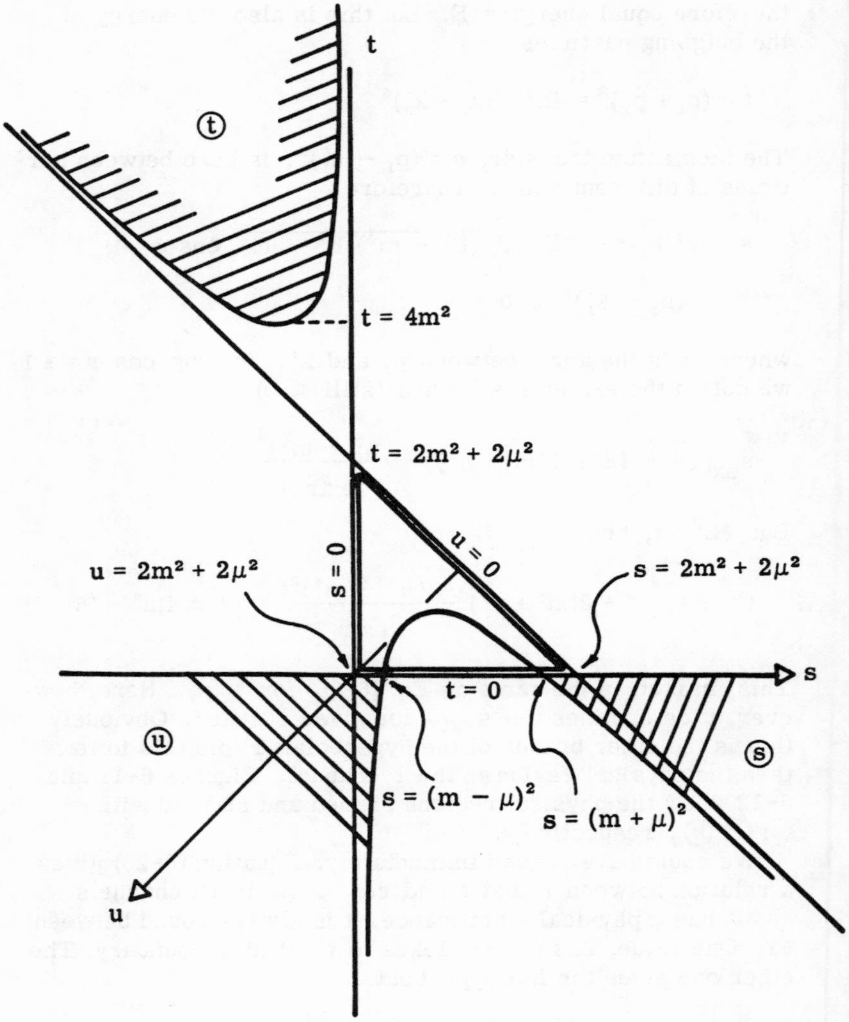

Fig. 6-12 Physical regions of s, t, u channels in Cartesian st plane for $m > \mu$.

Problem:

6-2. The dispersion relation for $\pi - N$ scattering in the model case, where both particles are neutral and scalar, takes the following form in the CM system:

$$\operatorname{Re} T(s,t) = g\left(\frac{1}{s + t - m^2 - 2\mu^2} - \frac{1}{s - m^2}\right)$$

$$+ \frac{1}{\pi} P \int_{(m+\mu)^2}^{\infty} ds' \operatorname{Im} T(s',t) \tag{6-28}$$

$$\times \left(\frac{1}{s' + t - 2(m^2 + \mu^2) + s} + \frac{1}{s' - s}\right)$$

[For a derivation of this formula see, e.g., "Introduction to Field Theory and Dispersion Relations," R. Hagedorn, *Fortschr. Phys*., 5. Sonderband (1963), Eq. (108).] Derive from this the forward dispersion relation in the lab. system, where the energy ω of the incoming pion serves as variable.

Solution to 6-2:

(a) Forward dispersion relation means $t = 0$. This holds in the CM system as well as in the lab. system.

(b) We evaluate in the lab. system ($\mathbf{p}_1 = 0$)

$$s = (p_1 + k_1)^2 = p_1^2 + k_1^2 + 2p_1k_1 = m^2 + \mu^2 + 2m\omega \tag{6-29}$$

where ω is the pion energy.

(c) Putting $t = 0$ and inserting $s = m^2 + \mu^2 + 2m\omega$; $ds' = 2m\, d\omega'$ immediately gives

$$\operatorname{Re} T(\omega) = \frac{g}{2m}\left(\frac{1}{\omega - \frac{\mu^2}{2m}} - \frac{1}{\omega + \frac{\mu^2}{2m}}\right)$$

$$+ \frac{1}{\pi} P \int_{\mu}^{\infty} d\omega' \operatorname{Im} T(\omega')$$

$$\times \left(\frac{1}{\omega' + \omega} + \frac{1}{\omega' - \omega}\right) \tag{6-30}$$

Further details on the physical regions, where the masses of all four particles are different, can be found in the article by T. W. B. Kibble, *Phys. Rev.*, **117**, 1159 (1960).

7

PHASE-SPACE CONSIDERATIONS

In this chapter we leave the narrow field of pure kinematics because the significance of phase space can be understood only by considering a physical system as a whole. It then turns out that the description can be split roughly into two parts, one of which describes the dynamical aspect and the other the kinematical aspect. The more particles participating in the process, the more the kinematical aspect tends to dominate the behavior of the system. This situation reaches the extreme in classical thermodynamics, where it has been possible to derive the phenomenological laws from statistical mechanics. There, in statistical mechanics, the dynamical part is the interaction between the particles—e.g., by van der Waals' forces—their internal structure and their ability to dissociate or combine in various manners. All the rest is kinematics, and the description of the kinematics is done by means of phase space. It turns out, then, that the kinematical description of the system leads to thermodynamics, formulated in terms of general laws relating temperature, volume, pressure, phase (gas, liquid, solid), chemical equilibrium, and so on. The form of these laws is quite general and does not depend on the dynamics in the sense defined above. The dynamics enter into these laws only by determining certain constants or parameters which are typical to the material that makes up the system. Such constants are, for instance, those appearing in van der Waals' equation (or similar, more refined ones), the specific heat equation, and others. Only when the large number of degrees of freedom is reduced—either by observing a small number of particles or by observing at very low temperatures—can the dynamical aspects become important enough to influence the form of the laws instead of only the values of some parameters in a given law.

In elementary particle quantum physics we are dealing with this latter situation. Either we consider a description in terms of nonrelativistic quantum mechanics and find only a few particles participating; or we consider a description by means of field theory and find an infinite number of degrees of freedom but observe "at extremely low temperatures" where most of them are frozen in. These nonexcited degrees of freedom are, for instance, those many particle states, whose thresholds lie above the available energy.

Nevertheless, even here exists a phase space which describes the kinematical aspects of the process considered. We cannot, however, expect that it contains the whole description up to some parameters determined by dynamics. We must indeed expect that the form of phenomenological descriptions (essentially: total and differential cross sections, angular correlations, decay modes, etc.) depends on both, dynamics and kinematics, at the same time. It is an important problem then to separate these two influences from each other, since what we are—in elementary particle physics—mainly interested in, is the dynamics.

7-1 THE SIGNIFICANCE OF PHASE SPACE AND ITS DEFINITION

It is a commonly accepted belief today that the most detailed information which we possibly can have about the predictable results of any experiment is contained in the S matrix.

We prepare (in an idealized situation) a pure initial quantum state $|i\rangle$, which may be written as a definite superposition of states forming a complete orthonormal basis in the Hilbert space. This state $|i\rangle$ is prepared at time $-T$ such that the particles described by it are so far apart from each other that they do not yet interact, but move such that they will come near to each other and undergo mutual interactions at some much later time, $T \approx 0$, say. We then wait a very long time until they have left the space-time region of interaction and have become again free at $+T$. Whether we are able to calculate what has happened in this interaction (e.g., by integrating a Schrödinger equation or a set of field equations between $-T$ and $+T$) is a question of the degree of our understanding of the dynamics of the process. Independently of our ability (or disability as a matter of fact) to calculate the state $|i'\rangle$ which would result from this integration, we believe that this new state $|i'\rangle$ which developed out of $|i\rangle$ is related to $|i\rangle$ by a unitary transformation S (in the limit $T \to \infty$):

$$|i'\rangle = S|i\rangle \tag{7-1}$$

which means that S does not depend on what $|i\rangle$ was, i.e., if we had prepared $|j\rangle$ instead of $|i\rangle$, then $|j'\rangle = S|j\rangle$ would hold with the same S. According to quantum mechanics we can—assuming S to be known—calculate the probability to find at T a situation described by a final state $|f\rangle$, namely,

$$\begin{aligned} \text{Prob}\,(i \to f) &= |\langle f|i'\rangle|^2 \\ &= |\langle f|S|i\rangle|^2 \end{aligned} \tag{7-2}$$

The initial state $|i\rangle$ as well as the final one $|f\rangle$ might be many-particle states. Practically, in elementary particle physics, $|i\rangle$ is a two-particle state; but $|f\rangle$ is frequently a many-particle state, since most experiments are carried out at energies allowing particle production. Now $|i\rangle$ and $|f\rangle$ are assumed to be free-particle states of composite particles as well as elementary ones (where these terms have a meaning only with respect to a field theoretical description with a given set of fields which are *defined* to be elementary). Free-particle states can be fully described by giving the complete quantum state of each single particle, e.g., its four-momentum, spin, nucleon number, etc.

In the simplest case of neutral, scalar particles we would write, for instance,

$$\begin{aligned} |i\rangle &= |p_1 p_2\rangle \\ |i'\rangle &= S\,|p_1 p_2\rangle \\ |f\rangle &= |p_1' p_2' p_3' \cdots p_n'\rangle \end{aligned} \tag{7-3}$$

and (7-2) gives us the probability (density) that the two-particle state $|p_1 p_2\rangle$ leads by scattering to an n-particle state $|p_1' \cdots p_n'\rangle$ with well-defined four-momenta of each of the n particles:

$$P(i \to f) = |\langle p_1' \cdots p_n'|S|p_1 p_2\rangle|^2 \tag{7-4}$$

Comparing this to the situation of statistical mechanics, we see that it corresponds to a complete integration of the equations of motion of an n-particle system. In the extreme case of statistical mechanics this is an information much too detailed to be of any interest to us; it would provide us with position and momentum of each of some 10^{23} particles at any given time T, that is, with 6×10^{23} functions of T. What one does then is essentially to average over all the unwanted information in order to obtain weighted mean values of only a few quantities which have a macroscopic significance as energy, pressure, volume, velocity-distribution, etc. Some of these quantities correspond to those in the quantum physical problem, e.g., velocity distributions $w(v)\,dv$, telling us what the probability is that a given particle has a velocity between v and $(v + dv)$ no matter what the other $10^{23} - 1$ particles do. In elementary particle physics the momentum spectrum of any particle produced in (7-4) is the analogon.

In classical statistical mechanics the above-mentioned averaging is done by integrating over a certain region of the phase space. Exactly the same is to be done as soon as the full amount of information contained in (7-4) and resulting from a complete integration of the basic equations is either unwanted or not even available because S is not known.

In the first case one carries out the average in order to relate the theoretical result to a feasible experimental situation, i.e., it is technically impossible to determine $|p_1' \cdots p_n'\rangle$ when n becomes larger than a relatively low number, say 5 to 10 or so—particularly if there are neutral particles involved.

In the second case, if S is not or not well known, one integrates over the details because one knows that then the whole content of S will boil down to a few parameters governing the more "macroscopic" description (probability distribution of the number n of particles in $|f\rangle$, momentum spectrum of one particle, etc.). Either the restricted knowledge on S may suffice to calculate these parameters or one determines them from experiments and obtains a restricted knowledge on S. This is what one does in a statistical theory of the type of Fermi's.

Let us now define what we mean by the phase space (or better, phase-space factor). For details see the standard textbooks (e.g., J. M. Jauch and F. Rohrlich, *The Theory of Photons and Electrons*, Addison-Wesley, Reading, Mass., 1955; J. Schweber, *Relativistic Quantum Field Theory*, 1961; etc.).

We know that the S matrix is invariant under the Lorentz group. That amounts to saying that the probability for a transition per unit time and unit volume must contain a factor $\delta^4(P_i - P_f)$ where $P_i = p_1 + p_2$; $P_f = p_1' + \cdots p_n'$. This guarantees four-momentum conservation. Instead of talking of a transition probability per unit time and unit volume we may equally well speak of the transition probability "per event," since both are proportional to each other; the factor of proportionality depends on the flux (density and velocity) of the incoming particles and is presently of no interest for us.

Let now F be a set of final states $|f\rangle$, namely,

$$F = \{|f\rangle\} \tag{7-5}$$

of which we leave open at present how it is defined.

Disregarding any normalization factor (flux, etc.) we see, then, that the probability (e.g., per event) that the initial state $|i\rangle$ goes over into *any one* state $|f\rangle$ of the set F is given by

$$P(i \to F) \propto \sum_{f \in F} |\langle f | S | i \rangle|^2 \tag{7-6}$$

Since the final states were chosen to be described by the four-momenta p_i' of the particles the sum $\Sigma_{f \in F}$ is to be taken as a symbol for a restricted integral over these final momenta. Taking out the $\delta^4(P_i - P_f)$ and defining a function

$$S(p_1' \cdots p_n' \mid p_1 p_2) \equiv \delta^4(p_1' + p_2' + \cdots p_n' - p_1 - p_2) \times |\langle p_1' \cdots p_n' | S | p_1 p_2 \rangle|^2 \tag{7-7}$$

we obtain

$$P(i \to F) \propto \underbrace{\int d^4 p_1' \int d^4 p_2' \cdots \int d^4 p_n'}_{\text{integrated over F}} \times \delta^4(p_1' + p_2' + \cdots p_n' - p_1 - p_2) \times \prod_{i=1}^{n} \delta(p_i'^2 - m_i^2)\, S(p_1' \cdots p_n' | p_1 p_2) \tag{7-8}$$

Here the factor $\Pi_{i=1}^{n} \delta(p_i'^2 - m_i^2)$ has been introduced for convenience. Since the probability is a relativistic invariant and the function S is invariant, the other factors have to be invariant too. This can be done by integrating over the outgoing four-momenta with a δ function which fixes the mass value; or it can be done by integrating over three-momenta only and adding a further factor $\Pi_{i=1}^{n}(2p_{0i}')^{-1}$—both procedures are equivalent (see problem 5-1). The set of final states considered, F, may be any domain in this 4n-fold integral. For instance, F may be infinitesimal in all three-momenta:

$$F = \{p_1' \cdots p_n';\ d^3 p_1' \cdots d^3 p_n'\} \tag{7-9}$$

In this case $P(i \to F)$ would be zero because of the $\delta^4(P_i - P_f)$ except if $p_1' \cdots p_n'$ had been chosen to fulfil four-momentum conservation. In this latter case $P(i \to F)$ would be proportional to the "most differential" cross section which exists in our simple final state of neutral scalar particles.

Leaving F unrestricted but for one single momentum, namely,

$$F = \{p_1'; d^3p_1'\} \tag{7-10}$$

would lead to the momentum spectrum of particle 1; specifying two three-momenta gives angular correlations, etc. If F is not restricted whatsoever, $P(i \to F)$ simply yields a number proportional to the partial cross section for the production of n particles.

In Eq. (7-8) we see that the dynamical aspects of the process are contained in the function $S(p_1' \cdots p_n' | p_1 p_2)$, whereas all the rest is pure kinematics. This rest is called the "phase-space factor,"

$$R_F \equiv \underbrace{\int \cdots \int}_{F} \prod_{i=1}^{n} \delta(p_i'^2 - m_i^2)$$

$$\times\ \delta^4(p_1' + p_2' + \cdots p_n' - p_1 - p_2)\, d^4p_1' \cdots d^4p_n' \tag{7-11}$$

and F is called a "region of phase space." If F is defined in an invariant way, R_F is a relativistic invariant. If there is no restriction on the range F of integration, R certainly is an invariant, which then is called the "phase-space integral."

[*Remark:* Sometimes R_F is called the "momentum-space factor" because it contains only momentum integrations, whereas in analogy to the phase space of statistical mechanics there should be also space integrations. In fact, if one chooses to normalize the wave functions in a box of volume V, there will appear a factor V^n corresponding to an n-fold integral over V. But since this factor has to disappear as soon as one arrives at the explicit form of any measurable quantity (probability, cross section, etc.) we may forget about it altogether. In this sense we may call R_F the "phase-space factor" although the word "momentum-space factor" may be more adequate. Sometimes it is also defined with an additional factor $(h)^{-3n} = (2\pi\hbar)^{-3n} = (2\pi)^{-3n}$ ($\hbar = 1$ in our units). The meaning of this is that it then counts "the number of states" of n particles enclosed in a box of volume V and subject to four-momentum conservation. To make this number a relativistic invariant, V has to be defined in an invariant way, e.g., by saying that V is to be chosen in any Lorentz system such that by an L transformation to the over-all center-of-momentum frame it becomes equal to V_{CM}. All these small variations in the definition of "momentum space" or "phase space" are of no importance for us here. From now on we shall consistently use our definition and the name "phase space."

7-2 THE STATISTICAL THEORY

The statistical theory was invented by E. Fermi [*Progr. Theoret. Phys.*, **5**, 570 (1950)] along the following arguments:

1. The kind of prediction about an n-particle production process which one normally wishes to calculate is much less detailed than what could be obtained if $S(p_1' \cdots p_n' \mid p_1 p_2)$ would be known.
2. It is well known from statistical mechanics and intuitively obvious that by integrating over a large region (F) of the phase space, the dynamical details are averaged out and only a few typical parameters remain.
3. Actually nobody is able to calculate $S(p_1' \cdots p_n' \mid p_1 p_2)$. However, because of the first two arguments, this will not be necessary. A rather restricted knowledge on S may still lead to sensible results.

In most cases one wishes to know two things: the total probability for an n-particle final state, and the momentum spectrum of the particles. Therefore the first point of these arguments is met in practice.

Let us now write down what (7-8) answers to these questions (assume only one type of particles). Probability for n particles being present at the end:

$$P_n \propto \int \cdots \int \prod_{i=1}^{n} d^4 p_i' \, \delta(p_i'^2 - m^2)$$

$$\times\, \delta^4\left(\sum_{j=1}^{n} p_j' - p_1 - p_2\right) S(p_1' \cdots p_n' \mid p_1 p_2)$$

$$\equiv \bar{S}_n \underbrace{\int \cdots \int \prod_{i=1}^{n} d^4 p_i' \, \delta(p_i'^2 - m^2)\, \delta^4\left(\sum_j p_j' - p_1 - p_2\right)}_{R_n}$$

$$\equiv \bar{S}_n R_n \tag{7-12}$$

Iere $\overline{S}_n$ is defined by the equation to be the weighted average of the -particle S function, taken over the whole phase space. Apart rom the initial state (which we consider to be fixed) this average lepends only on n, and it is conceivable that the details of the inter-ction will not have a great influence on the behavior of $\overline{S}_n$ as a unction of n (except for small n). What presumably will determine his function of n are the strength and range of interaction. This is oint two of Fermi's idea.

The second question concerns the momentum spectrum of the articles produced. We may choose particle 1 to represent this pectrum; we take $F = \{p_1'; d^3p_1'\}$ and obtain

$$W(p_1')\, d^3p_1' \propto d^3p_1 \int_F \cdots \int \delta(p_1'^2 - m^2)\, dp_{01} \prod_{i=2}^{n} \delta(p_i'^2 - m^2)$$

$$\times\, d^4p_i'\, \delta^4\left(\sum_{j=1}^{n} p_j' - p_1 - p_2\right) S(p_1' \cdots p_n' \,|\, p_1 p_2)$$

$$\equiv d^3p_1'\, \overline{S}_n(p_1') R_F \tag{7-13}$$

Iere the situation is different in so far as the average $\overline{S}_n(p_1')$ now epends not only on n but also on $\mathbf{p}_1$. The phase-space factor, owever, depends not on the vector $\mathbf{p}_1$ but only on its magnitude, s soon as we choose the over-all center-of-momentum frame for he description. That is so because, in the CM frame, the only actor in R_F where a dependence of the direction of $\mathbf{p}_1$ occurs, is

$$\delta^4\left(\sum_{j=1}^{n} p_j' - p_1 - p_2\right)$$

$$= \delta\left(\sum_{j=1}^{n} E_j - E_{CM}\right) \delta^3\left(\sum_{j=1}^{n} \mathbf{p}_j'\right) \tag{7-14}$$

ince there $\mathbf{p}_1 + \mathbf{p}_2 = 0$. Now in the δ^3 function we integrate over all $- 1$ momenta $\mathbf{p}_2' \cdots \mathbf{p}_n'$ and therefore the direction of $\mathbf{p}_1'$ is ir-elevant.

There may be cases where a dynamical model is available which ays how $\overline{S}_n(p_1')$ depends on $\mathbf{p}_1'$ [which is already much less than he knowledge of $S(p_1' \cdots p_n' \,|\, p_1 p_2)$]. If that is not so then one may till average over all directions of $\mathbf{p}_1'$, taking advantage of R_F

being independent of these directions. The result is essentially a kinetic-energy spectrum:

$$\overline{W}(|p_i'|) \propto |p_i'|^2 \, d|p_i'|\overline{\overline{S}}_n(|p_i'|)R_F \tag{7-15}$$

One may now say that perhaps the dependence of the double average $\overline{\overline{S}}_n(|p_i'|)$ is so smooth and slow that the kinematical factor $|p_i'|^2 R_F$ essentially determines the spectrum. In that case $\overline{\overline{S}}_n(|p_i'|)$ can be replaced by a constant which is (up to some factor 4π) our old $\overline{S}_n$. Then the spectrum $\overline{W}$ is given entirely by $|p_i'|^2 R_F$, that is, by the pure "phase-space factor." This simplification works surprisingly well in some cases (pion kinetic-energy spectra in pp collisions at $\lesssim 30$ GeV) and very badly in others (nucleon spectra in pp collisions at $\lesssim 30$ GeV).

We cannot discuss here the physics involved—we can only state that the phase-space factor already contains a certain amount of information. The influence of the dynamical aspects become less important the more we average, or, in other words, the larger the region F of integration becomes.

In order to obtain an idea of what $\overline{S}_n$ might be, we consider the inverse process: n particles move toward a space-time region of mutual interaction, join, and yield two particles with high energy. In this inverse reaction the final state is fixed. We must, however, now average over all those initial states (now n-particle states) which can give contributions to the inverse processes, namely, all those contained in the set F. The S-matrix element squared is the same—only what has been an integration over the former final states (namely, F) has now to be replaced by taking the average over the present initial states (namely, F again). This average was by definition just our $\overline{S}_n$. Hence—without any further phase-space factor —

$$P(F \to i) \propto \overline{S}_n \tag{7-16}$$

Now we discuss the statistical argument which settles point three of Fermi's idea. Assume the n particles to be created from an intermediate state of "statistical equilibrium"; then, if normalized in a box of volume V, the end state will also reflect this equilibrium. Hence in considering the inverse process we should assume the n particles to be in "thermodynamical" equilibrium in a box of volume V. Then the probability that they will all join at the same time in a small volume Ω (whose radius equals the range of interaction, e.g., $\sim 1/m_\pi$) is proportional to $(\Omega/V)^n$. Hence

$$\overline{S}_n \propto \left(\frac{\Omega}{V}\right)^n \qquad \Omega \approx \frac{4\pi}{3}\left(\frac{1}{m_\pi}\right)^3 \tag{7-17}$$

Here the V^n drops against a factor V^n contained in the phase-space factor (see the *Remark* earlier in the chapter). This $\overline{S}_n$ may then be inserted into formulas (7-12 and 7-15).†

This is the main idea of the statistical theory. For refinements and applications see, e.g., the articles by M. Kretzschmar [*Ann. Rev. Nucl. Sci.*, **11**, 1 (1961)] and R. Hagedorn [*Nuovo Cimento*, **15**, 434 (1960) and **25**, 1017 (1962)] and literature quoted there.

It should be clear, from this discussion, that one cannot expect any precision from a statistical theory and that one should even sometimes expect seriously wrong results, because the particle numbers are not large and the dynamical aspects have been oversimplified. [See, e.g., the critical review by R. Hagedorn, *CERN*, **61-62**, 183 (1961).]

But even then, studying the phase-space factor is worthwhile, particularly if not too many particles are involved. The phase-space factor yields a background (in fact, the behavior of the system which one would find, if the matrix element would be constant) from which every significant dynamic property should exhibit itself clearly. It is in this sense that one uses it frequently in elementary particle physics.

7-3 INVARIANT AND NONINVARIANT PHASE SPACE

Let us go back to Eq. (7-12) and use the formula (5-24),

$$\delta(p^2 - m^2) = \frac{\delta(p_0 + \varepsilon) + \delta(p_0 - \varepsilon)}{2\varepsilon} \qquad \varepsilon = \sqrt{p^2 + m^2}$$

in order to carry out the integration over p'_{0i} (which by physical reasons is restricted to $p'_{0i} \geq 0$). We obtain in the CM frame

$$P_n \propto \int \cdots \int d^3p'_1 \cdots d^3p'_n \, \delta(E_{CM} - \Sigma \varepsilon'_i)$$

$$\times \delta^3(\Sigma p'_i) \frac{S(p'_1 \cdots p'_n \mid p_1 p_2)}{\Pi_{i=1}^n \, 2\varepsilon'_i} \tag{7-18}$$

If we now take the mean value of $S(p'_1 \cdots p'_n \mid p_1 p_2)$ in front of the

---

†The proportionality (7-17) includes a factor $\{\overline{[\Pi_{i=1}^n \, 2\varepsilon'_i]^{-1}}\}^{-1}$, as follows from the discussion in the next section [see Eq. (7-20)].

integral, we obtain again our old formula $P_n \propto \overline{S}_n R_n$ with the only difference that in R_n the p'_{oi} integrations have been carried out (in the CM frame).

We could, however, in a second step, take also the mean value of

$$\left[\prod_{i=1}^{n} 2\varepsilon'_i\right]^{-1}$$

in front of the integral. Calling the product of the two mean values $\overline{S'_n}$:

$$\overline{\left[\prod_{i=1}^{n} 2\varepsilon'_i\right]^{-1}} \cdot \overline{S}_n \equiv \overline{S'_n} \tag{7-19}$$

we see that in the center-of-momentum frame two equivalent descriptions emerge:

$$P_n \propto \overline{S}_n R_n = \overline{S}_n \overline{\left[\prod_{i=1}^{n} 2\varepsilon'_i\right]^{-1}} \times \rho_n = \overline{S'}_n \rho_n \tag{7-20}$$

In this particular frame of reference both descriptions are the same; but whereas $\overline{S}_n$ and R_n were separately Lorentz-invariant, this is not so in the other description. There only the product of $\overline{S'_n}$ and ρ_n is invariant, not each factor. In addition to that the dimensions of $\overline{S}_n$ and $\overline{S'_n}$ and those of R_n and ρ_n also differ, by a factor† $(\text{energy})^n$.

Explicitly then, we have (in the general case of different masses) the two definitions of phase space:

Invariant phase space R_n:

$$R_n(P, m_1 \cdots m_n) = \int \cdots \int \prod_{i=1}^{n} d^4 p_i \; \delta(p_i^2 - m_i^2) \times \delta^4\left(\sum_{j=1}^{n} p_j - P\right) \tag{7-21a}$$

where P is the total four momentum of the whole system.

---

†Numerical estimates of this factor may be obtained from $\overline{[\Pi_{i=1}^n 2\varepsilon'_i]^{-1}} \approx \{\overline{[\Pi_{i=1}^n 2\varepsilon'_i]}\}^{-1}$; $\overline{[\Pi_{i=1}^n 2\varepsilon'_i]} \approx 2^n \Pi_{i=1}^n \overline{\varepsilon'_i}$. Here $\overline{\varepsilon'_i}$ may be calculated from the assumption of equipartition of ***kinetic*** energies: $\overline{\varepsilon'_i} \approx m_i + (E - \Sigma_{j=1}^n m_j)/n$.

Noninvariant phase space ρ_n (in the CM frame of the system):

$$\rho_n(E, m_1 \cdots m_n) = \int \cdots \int \delta\left(E - \sum_{i=1}^{n} \varepsilon_i\right) \times \delta^3(\Sigma \mathbf{p}_i)\, d^3p_1 \cdots d^3p_n \qquad (7\text{-}21b)$$

where E is the total CM energy of the whole system and $\varepsilon_i = \sqrt{\mathbf{p}_i^2 + m_i^2}$ is the energy of particle i.

Fermi has formulated his statistical theory in terms of the noninvariant phase space† ρ_n, which since then has been used until today. It becomes, however, more and more customary to use the invariant phase space both in statistical theory calculations and in finding the "background" from which dynamical properties should exhibit themselves. The remarkable advantages of the invariant phase space have been first pointed out by P. P. Shrivastava and E. C. G. Sudarshan [*Phys. Rev.*, **110**, 765 (1958)]. In high-energy physics, where one systematically tries to formulate everything in a covariant or invariant way, the invariant phase space is the only relevant one for general considerations. As soon, however, as one definitely sticks to the center-of-momentum frame, the noninvariant phase space can be used equally well.

Both forms of the phase space have a common drawback: as long as the relativistic formula $\varepsilon_i = \sqrt{\mathbf{p}_i^2 + m_i^2}$ for the energy of the particles must be used, the phase-space integrals cannot be calculated analytically for more than three particles; numerical integration is unavoidable. Analytical formulas can be obtained if either of the limiting cases,

$$\sqrt{\mathbf{p}_i^2 + m_i^2} \nearrow |\mathbf{p}_i| \qquad \text{ultrarelativistic}$$

$$\sqrt{\mathbf{p}_i^2 + m_i^2} \searrow m_i + \frac{|\mathbf{p}_i|^2}{2m_i} \qquad \text{nonrelativistic}$$

is reached for each particle in the integral.

Numerical integrations are simpler in the invariant phase space because the Lorentz invariance leads to a recurrence formula. Let us separate out the last (n^{th}) integration in (7-21a):

---

†It is $\overline{S}'_n$ to which the consideration leading to (7-17) applies more directly: $\overline{S}'_n \approx (\Omega/V)^n$.

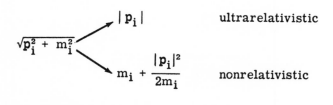

$$R_n(P, m_1 \cdots m_n) = \int \prod_{i=1}^{n} \delta(p_i^2 - m_i^2)\, d^4 p_i$$

$$\times\, \delta^4\left(\sum_{j=1}^{n-1} p_j - (P - p_n)\right)$$

$$\times\, \delta(p_n^2 - m_n^2)\, d^4 p_n$$

The first factor is by definition $R_{n-1}(P - p_n;\ m_1 \cdots m_{n-1})$; hence with $\delta(p_n^2 - m_n^2)\, d^4 p_n \rightarrow d^3 p_n / 2E_n$,

$$R_n(P, m_1 \cdots m_n) = \int \frac{d^3 p_n}{2E_n} R_{n-1}\,(P - p_n;\ m_1 \cdots m_{n-1}) \tag{7-22a}$$

We now use the relativistic invariance to calculate R_n in the CM system $[P = (E, 0)]$ and R_{n-1} in the system where

$$P - p_n = (\varepsilon, 0) \qquad \varepsilon^2 = (P - p_n)^2 = (E - E_n)^2 - (\mathbf{P} - \mathbf{p}_n)^2$$
$$= (E - E_n)^2 - \mathbf{p}_n^2$$

(where we have calculated the invariant $\varepsilon^2 = (P - p_n)^2$ in the CM frame). Hence with $E_n^2 = \mathbf{p}_n^2 + m_n^2$ we obtain the recurrence formula

$$R_n(E; m_1 \cdots m_n)$$
$$= \int \frac{d^3 p_n}{2\sqrt{\mathbf{p}_n^2 + m_n^2}}$$
$$\times\, R_{n-1}\left(\sqrt{E^2 + m_n^2 - 2E\sqrt{\mathbf{p}_n^2 + m_n^2}}\,;\ m_1 \cdots m_{n-1}\right) \tag{7-22b}$$

To start with, one may define a one-particle phase space, evaluated in the rest system of the particle. Equation (7-21a) gives

$$R_1(E; m) = \int \frac{d^3 p}{2\sqrt{\mathbf{p}^2 + m^2}}\ \delta(E - \sqrt{\mathbf{p}^2 + m^2})\ \delta^3(\mathbf{p})$$
$$= \frac{\delta(E - m)}{2m} \tag{7-22c}$$

One could also start from a direct calculation of the two-body phase space; this will be done in Section 7-6c, where we need R_2 explicitly.

> *Exercise:* Calculate $R_2(a;b,c)$ using the recurrence formula (7-22b) and R_1 from (7-22c) and check the result with (7-57).

A similar formula could be derived for expressing ρ_n by an integral over ρ_{n-1}. However, because ρ is not invariant, ρ_{n-1} in the integral is taken with nonzero total momentum, which makes it much more complicated and impracticable.

Still another type of recurrence formula, namely, (7-25), will be found in the next section when we consider the mass distribution. We shall not go into further details on computation here; they may be found in the literature on the statistical theory (see, e.g., the review article by M. Kretzschmar, quoted on p. 89).

7-4 MASS DISTRIBUTION

We shall now discuss a striking example, namely, the discovery of the ω meson, of how a dynamical property of a system exhibits itself from the background of "pure phase space." We shall use the invariant phase space.

Consider the following situation: In a certain process n particles make up the final state. Let us divide these n particles into two groups (see Fig. 7-1), one with particles $i = 1 \cdots \ell$ $(\ell < n)$, the other containing the rest. Each group has a total four-momentum and rest mass:

$$P_\ell = \sum_{i=1}^{\ell} p_i \qquad M_\ell^2 = P_\ell^2$$
$$P_{n-\ell} = \sum_{i=\ell+1}^{n} p_i \qquad M_{n-\ell}^2 = P_{n-\ell}^2 \tag{7-23}$$

We now ask: What is, if everything is governed by pure phase space, the probability that the square of the rest mass M_ℓ^2 lies between M^2 and $M^2 + dM^2$? The answer to this question is a "mass distribution" which we shall calculate from the phase space. If this mass distribution is compared to the experimental one, any significant deviation has to be interpreted as an indication for a dynamical irregularity.

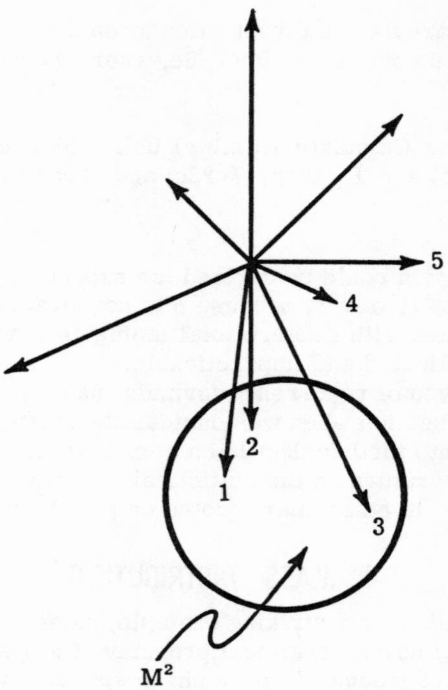

Fig. 7-1 Definition of the invariant mass of $\ell = 3$ particles.

We now calculate this mass distribution. We can easily split up the invariant phase space (7-21a)

$$R_n(P, m_1 \cdots m_n) = \int \cdots \int \prod_{i=1}^{n} \delta(p_i^2 - m_i^2) \times d^4 p_i \; \delta^4\left(\sum_{j=1}^{n} p_j - P\right)$$

into two parts by observing that

$$\delta(x - y) = \int \delta(x - z)\, \delta(z - y)\, dz$$

Doing this with the $\delta^4(\Sigma\, p_j - P)$, we may write

$$\delta^4\left(\sum_{j=1}^{n} p_j - P\right) = \int d^4 P_\ell \; \delta^4\left(P - P_\ell - \sum_{j=\ell+1}^{n} p_j\right)$$

$$\times \delta^4\left(P_\ell - \sum_{j=1}^{\ell} p_\ell\right)$$

and obtain

$$R_n(P,m_1 \cdots m_n)$$

$$= \int \delta^4\left(P - P_\ell - \sum_{j=\ell+1}^{n} p_j\right) \prod_{j=\ell+1}^{n} \delta\left(p_j^2 - m_j^2\right) d^4 p_j$$

$$\times \int \delta^4\left(P_i - \sum_{j=1}^{\ell} p_\ell\right) \prod_{j=1}^{\ell} \delta\left(p_j^2 - m_j^2\right) d^4 p_j \; d^4 P_\ell$$

This is not yet the splitting we need, because there is one four-momentum integration—that over P_ℓ—which is not accompanied by a factor $\delta(P_\ell^2 - M_\ell^2)$ corresponding to the similar factors of the other integrations. Therefore we introduce a factor 1 of the form

$$1 = \int_0^\infty \delta\left(P_\ell^2 - M^2\right) dM^2$$

and get

$$R_n(P;m_1 \cdots m_n)$$

$$= \int_0^\infty dM^2 \int \delta^4\left(P - P_\ell - \sum_{\ell+1}^{n} p_j\right) \prod_{\ell+1}^{n} \delta\left(p_j^2 - m_j^2\right)$$

$$\times \delta\left(P_\ell^2 - M^2\right) d^4 p_j \; d^4 P_\ell \int \delta^4\left(P_\ell - \sum_{1}^{\ell} p_j\right)$$

$$\times \prod_{1}^{\ell} \delta\left(p_j^2 - m_j^2\right) d^4 p_j \qquad (7\text{-}24)$$

According to the definition (7-21a) of R_n, this is a convolution integral over two invariant phase-space integrals and therefore a general recurrence formula:

$$R_n(P;m_1 \cdots m_n) = \int_0^\infty dM^2\, R_{n-\ell+1}(P;M,m_{\ell+1} \cdots m_n) \times R_\ell(P_\ell;m_1 \cdots m_\ell) \tag{7-25}$$

[actually the lower limit in the M^2 integration is $(\Sigma_1^\ell m_j)^2$]. The physical meaning of (7-25) is obvious (see Fig. 7-1).

$R_{n-\ell+1}(P;M,m_{\ell+1} \cdots m_n)$ describes the situation in which there are $n-1$ particles $m_{\ell+1} \cdots m_n$ plus one "particle" with mass $M = P_\ell^2$ representing the system of particles $m_1 \cdots m_\ell$ as one single kinematical object.

$R_\ell(P_\ell;m_1 \cdots m_\ell)$ describes the internal situation of the "particle" with total four momentum P_ℓ, which is made up by particles $m_1 \cdots m_\ell$.

Equation (7-25) is already the complete answer to the question of mass distribution: Because $R_n(P;m_1 \cdots m_\ell)$ is to be considered as a simple constant, we may divide by it and obtain

$$\int_0^\infty dM^2\, \frac{R_{n-\ell+1}(P;M,m_{\ell+1} \cdots m_n)\, R_\ell(P_\ell;m_1 \cdots m_\ell)}{R_n(P;m_1 \cdots m_n)} = 1 \tag{7-26}$$

from which it follows that the probability distribution $P(M)\, dM^2$ is given by

$$P(M)\, dM^2 = \frac{R_{n-\ell+1}(P;M,m_{\ell+1} \cdots m_n)\, R_\ell(P_\ell;m_1 \cdots m_\ell)}{R_n(P;m_1 \cdots m_n)}\, dM^2 \tag{7-27}$$

We may now take still advantage of the relativistic invariance of R_m (m any integer) to calculate each of the three R's (in fact R_n as a normalization constant may be neglected) in its own rest system:

$R_{n-\ell+1}(P;M,m_{\ell+1} \cdots m_n)$ may be evaluated in the overall center-of-momentum frame, where $P = (E_{CM},0)$

$R_\ell(P_\ell;m_1 \cdots m_\ell)$ may be evaluated in the rest system of the group of particles $j = 1 \cdots \ell$, where $P_\ell = (M,0)$.

[The reader who wishes to see explicitly the advantages of the invariant over the noninvariant phase space, may try to derive a formula corresponding to (7-25) by means of ρ_n. He will meet with great difficulties.

It should be mentioned that the general recurrence formula (7-25

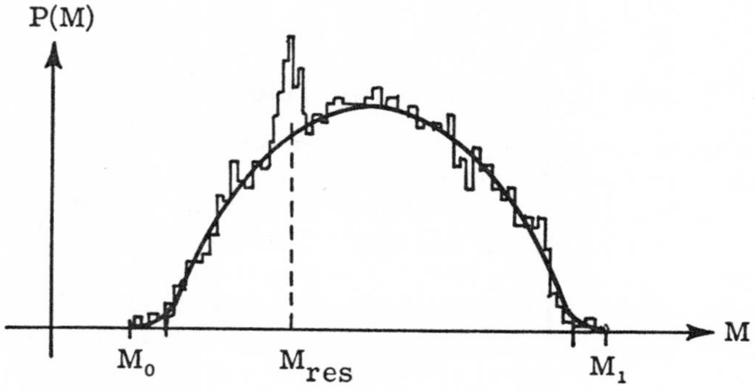

Fig. 7-2 The invariant mass distribution (smooth line) and typical experimental values when a resonance is present (histogram).

may also be used for numerical calculations of R_n. In particular if R_n for one large n is wanted and the complete sequence $R_2 R_3 \cdots R_n$ is not needed. Then one may proceed as suggested by (7-25): Put $n = 2m + 1$; $\ell = m + 1$; hence $R_{2m+1} = \int R_{m+1} R_{m+1}\, dM^2$, which, if only R's which have already been calculated are used, leads to the sequence $m = 1, 2, 4, 8, 16 \cdots$ or $R_3, R_5, R_9, R_{17}, R_{33} \cdots$. Intermediate R's may be again found with (7-25).]

The general form of the mass distribution (7-27) is clear: It becomes zero at the two limits where $M = M_0 = m_1 + m_2 + \cdots + m_\ell$ and where $M = M_1 = E_{CM} - m_{\ell+1} - \cdots - m_n$ and is positive in between. We expect therefore something like Fig. 7-2. The ω meson has been discovered in this way: An experimental histogram of the mass distribution of three pions with total charge zero was compared to the mass distribution (7-27) and a sharp peak like the one in Fig. 7-2 was found. This is then interpreted as an unstable bound state of three mesons and called the "ω meson." From the width of the peak one can conclude that the lifetime is of the order of 10^{-22} sec. That means that this particle would fly not much farther than 10^{-12} cm even if it had a velocity of the order of the velocity of light! It would be hard to observe such a particle directly; the deviations from pure phase space have lead to its discovery. [For further details see the article by B. C. Maglic, L. W. Alvarez, A. H. Rosenfeld, and M. L. Stevenson, *Phys. Rev. Lett.*, **7**, 178 (1961).]

7-5 THE DALITZ PLOT

A. The Energy Distribution from Pure Kinematics

In the technique of the Dalitz plot one looks again for the deviations of an experimental distribution of points from what pure phase space would predict. From these deviations one can conclude something about the structure of the matrix element. This technique has been applied with success to the ω meson, for example.

This idea is this: After the mass distribution showed a striking deviation from pure phase-space predictions for P(M), one selects all those three-pion states which have $M^2 = M^2_{res} = M^2_\omega$ and sees what the pure phase space has to predict about its mode of decay.

Let $p_i = (E_i, \mathbf{p}_i)$ be the four-momenta of the three pions in $\omega \to \pi + \pi + \pi$. The "differential invariant phase space," predicting the momentum distribution on the basis of pure kinematics, is in the ω rest frame given by $(m_\pi = m)$:

$$d^9R(M; m,m,m) = \delta(M - E_1 - E_2 - E_3)\ \delta^3(\mathbf{p}_1 + \mathbf{p}_2 + \mathbf{p}_3) \times \frac{d^3p_1}{2E_1}\frac{d^3p_2}{2E_2}\frac{d^3p_3}{2E_3} \tag{7-28}$$

where [as in (7-18)] the p_0 integrations have been carried out with the effect of replacing $\delta(p^2 - m^2)\, d^4p$ by $d^3p/2E$.

This "differential phase space" d^9R_3 depends on three momenta that is, nine variables, whose range is restricted by four equations: $\mathbf{p}_1 + \mathbf{p}_2 + \mathbf{p}_3 = 0$ (three equations) and $M = E_1 + E_2 + E_3$. Hence it depends on five independent variables. If the number of available events is not large, it is impossible to obtain statistically significant results for five independent variables. One may then reduce the number of variables by integrating over the unwanted information. In this case—which leads to the Dalitz plot—one integrates over all angles and considers thus the energies E_1, E_2, E_3 of the three pions as the variables. Since $E_1 + E_2 + E_2 = M$, only two independent ones remain. This yields a much better statistics.

We ask therefore: What has the phase space to say about the distribution function of any two of the three energies, E_1 and E_2, say? Therefore we want $P(E_1E_2)\, dE_1\, dE_2$; we obtain it by suitable integrations on $d^9R(M,m,m,m)$.

We first integrate (7-28) over $\mathbf{p}_3$ with the result

$$d^6R = \frac{\delta(M - E_1 - E_2 - E_3)}{2E_3}\frac{d^3p_1}{2E_1}\frac{d^3p_2}{2E_2} \qquad E_3 = \sqrt{(\mathbf{p}_1 + \mathbf{p}_2)^2 + m^2} \tag{7-29}$$

Now $\mathbf{p}_1$ and $\mathbf{p}_2$ are arbitrary—the energy-δ function cares for energy conservation.

The next step is to integrate over the angles: first over the directions $\mathbf{p}_2$ relative to a fixed direction of $\mathbf{p}_1$, then over the directions of $\mathbf{p}_1$ itself. Call θ the angle between $\mathbf{p}_1$ and $\mathbf{p}_2$ and put $\cos\theta = \xi$. Then the first angular integration consists in replacing d^3p_2 by

$$2\pi p_2^2 \, dp_2 \, d\xi$$

and the second angular integration (because after the first integration no direction is distinguished any longer) in replacing d^3p_1 by

$$4\pi p_1^2 \, dp_1$$

Hence we obtain

$$d^2R = \int \frac{\delta(M - E_1 - E_2 - E_3)}{2E_3} \, 8\pi^2 \frac{p_1^2 p_2^2}{2E_1 2E_2} \, dp_1 \, dp_2 \, d\xi$$

$$E_3 = \sqrt{p_1^2 + p_2^2 + 2p_1p_2\xi + m^2} \qquad (7\text{-}30)$$

(Note that here p_i means $|\mathbf{p}_i|$ and not a four-vector.) We now transform the integral to the variables

$$E_1 = \sqrt{p_1^2 + m^2}$$

$$E_2 = \sqrt{p_2^2 + m^2}$$

$$E_3 = \sqrt{p_1^2 + p_2^2 + 2p_1p_2\xi + m^2}$$

by means of [see (5-7)]

$$dp_1 \, dp_2 \, d\xi = dE_1 \, dE_2 \, dE_3 \, \frac{\partial(p_1 p_2 \xi)}{\partial(E_1 E_2 E_3)}$$

The Jacobian is easily found to be

$$\frac{\partial(p_1 p_2 \xi)}{\partial(E_1 E_2 E_3)} = \left[\frac{\partial(E_1 E_2 E_3)}{\partial(p_1 p_2 \xi)}\right]^{-1} = \frac{E_1 E_2 E_3}{p_1^2 p_2^2}$$

Inserting this into the integral (7-30) yields

$$d^2R = \pi^2 \int \frac{\delta(M - E_1 - E_2 - E_3)}{E_1 E_2 E_3} \frac{E_1 E_2 E_3}{p_1^2 p_2^2} p_1^2 p_2^2 \, dE_1 \, dE_2 \, dE_3$$

$$= \pi^2 \int \delta(M - E_1 - E_2 - E_3) \, dE_1 \, dE_2 \, dE_3$$

$$= \pi^2 \, dE_1 \, dE_2$$

This is—up to an uninteresting normalization constant—the probability distribution we wish:

$$P(E_1 E_2) \, dE_1 \, dE_2 = \text{const.} \, dE_1 \, dE_2 \tag{7-31}$$

That is: $P(E_1 E_2)$ is constant and does not depend on E_1 and E_2 at all.

If we now plot the experimental distribution against a constant distribution, every deviation would be due to the matrix element—if we could be sure that all events we use to plot the experimental distribution are coming from genuine $\omega = 3\pi$ decay. Unfortunately we cannot be sure of that, because, as Fig. 7-2 shows, there is always a considerable background of 3π states which accidentally (i.e., for pure phase-space reasons) have just the mass M_ω: these are all those lying below the $P(M^2)$ curve in the peak region. They, of course, may have any kind of matrix elements, and significant deviations from the constant (E_1, E_2) distribution can come only from those which are contained in the peak above the $P(M^2)$ curve in Fig. 7-2. As far as the ω meson is concerned, this was in fact sufficient to determine spin and parity with a rather good reliability.

B. The Dalitz Triangle

The plot can be done in a very elegant way, a way that was first proposed by Dalitz [R. Dalitz, *Phil. Mag.*, **44**, 1068 (1953); see also E. Fabri, *Nuovo Cimento,* **11**, 479 (1954), whose notation we shall use in the following].

The idea is to plot not only E_1 and E_2 but all three energies E_1, E_2, and E_3. Since $E_1 + E_2 + E_3 = M_\omega$, we have of course only two independent variables. We know, however, from the Mandelstam diagram of the three variables s, t, u with $s + t + u = 4m^2$ that three such variables may be plotted in a plane if one interprets them to be the distances from three sides of a triangle (see Section 6-4). Dalitz does exactly the same. We shall present here the relativistic version of E. Fabri (quoted above). We choose an equilateral triangle of height $M - 3_m = Q = \varepsilon_1 + \varepsilon_2 + \varepsilon_3$ (Fig. 7-3), where

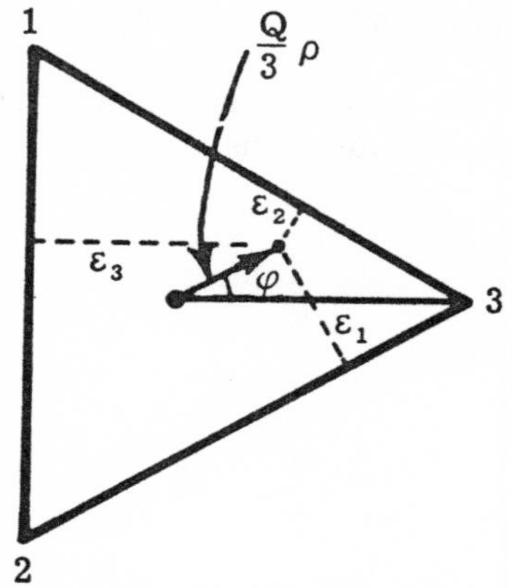

Fig. 7-3 The Dalitz triangle.

$\varepsilon_i = E_i - m$ are the kinetic energies and Q is the total kinetic energy.

Any point in the triangle can now be characterized by the three distances ε_1, ε_2, ε_3 from the sides, or, conveniently by polar coordinates; we introduce them as follows: if all three particles have the same kinetic energy, the representing point lies in the center of our triangle: $\varepsilon_1 = \varepsilon_2 = \varepsilon_3 = Q/3$. For all other points we measure the position by giving the distance ρ and the angle φ according to Fig. 7-3:

$$\varepsilon_1 = \frac{Q}{3}(1 + \rho \cos \varphi_1) \qquad \varphi_1 = \varphi - \frac{2\pi}{3}$$

$$\varepsilon_2 = \frac{Q}{3}(1 + \rho \cos \varphi_2) \qquad \varphi_2 = \varphi + \frac{2\pi}{3} \qquad (7\text{-}32)$$

$$\varepsilon_3 = \frac{Q}{3}(1 + \rho \cos \varphi) \qquad \varphi \text{ as in Fig. 7-3}$$

C. The Boundary Curve

The conservation of energy is guaranteed by the way of representing the points. The condition of momentum conservation is, however, not yet taken into account. It will imply a restriction on where the points representing events can lie. It is, for instance, clear that no event can lie in a corner of our triangle, because that would mean, e.g., $\varepsilon_1 = Q$, $\varepsilon_2 = \varepsilon_3 = 0$, which states that particles 2 and 3 are at rest and only 1 moves—in contradiction to $\mathbf{p}_1 + \mathbf{p}_2 + \mathbf{p}_3 = 0$.

We shall now derive the boundary curve outside of which no events can lie. From momentum conservation follows (p_1 stays for $|\mathbf{p}_i|$)

$$(\mathbf{p}_1 + \mathbf{p}_2)^2 = \mathbf{p}_3^2$$

$$p_1^2 + p_2^2 + 2p_1p_2 \cos\theta = p_3^2$$

Hence

$$4p_1^2p_2^2 \geq (p_1^2 + p_2^2 - p_3^2)^2 \tag{7-33}$$

The boundary curve is given implicitly by the equality sign in (7-33). To find an explicit expression we have to express (7-33) by means of our variables; $p_i^2 = E_i^2 - m^2 = \varepsilon_i^2 + 2m\varepsilon_i$ gives

$$4(\varepsilon_1^2 + 2m\varepsilon_1)(\varepsilon_2^2 + 2m\varepsilon_2) = [\varepsilon_1^2 + \varepsilon_2^2 - \varepsilon_3^2 + 2m(\varepsilon_1 + \varepsilon_2 - \varepsilon_3)]^2 \tag{7-34}$$

In this equation ε_1 and ε_2 can be eliminated, leaving only ε_3. Indeed, ε_1 and ε_2 occur only in the combinations

$$2\varepsilon_1\varepsilon_2 = (\varepsilon_1 + \varepsilon_2)^2 - (\varepsilon_1^2 + \varepsilon_2^2) \qquad \varepsilon_1 + \varepsilon_2 \qquad \text{and} \qquad \varepsilon_1^2 + \varepsilon_2^2$$

and combinations thereof. These expressions can be reduced to others containing only ε_3; this follows from (7-32), namely,

$$\varepsilon_1 + \varepsilon_2 + \varepsilon_3 = Q$$

which implies $\qquad \cos\varphi_1 + \cos\varphi_2 + \cos\varphi = 0$

$$\varepsilon_1^2 + \varepsilon_2^2 + \varepsilon_3^2 = \frac{Q^2}{9}[3 + \underbrace{2\rho(\cos\varphi_1 + \cos\varphi_2 + \cos\varphi)}_{=0}$$

$$+ \underbrace{\rho^2(\cos^2\varphi_1 + \cos^2\varphi_2 + \cos^2\varphi)}_{=\frac{3}{2}}]$$

Hence we have the relations

$$\varepsilon_1 + \varepsilon_2 + \varepsilon_3 = Q$$
$$\varepsilon_1^2 + \varepsilon_2^2 + \varepsilon_3^2 = \frac{Q^2}{3}(1 + \tfrac{1}{2}\rho^2) \tag{7-35}$$

With the help of these relations (7-34) may be rewritten such that it contains only ε_3, Q, ρ^2, and m, and since $\varepsilon_3 = (Q/3)(1 + \rho \cos \varphi)$ it becomes an equation between ρ, φ, Q, and m. A somewhat long procedure of multiplying out, squaring, and ordering of terms leads then to the expression

$$\rho^2[(4 - 2\sigma + \sigma^2) + 2\sigma\rho \cos 3\varphi] = (2 - \sigma)^2$$
$$\sigma \equiv Q/M \tag{7-36}$$

which can be brought to the form

$$\rho^2 = \frac{1}{1 + \dfrac{2\sigma}{(2 - \sigma)^2}(1 + \rho \cos 3\varphi)} \tag{7-37}$$

Points corresponding to physical events must lie always inside the boundary curve defined by (7-37). Note that ρ appears on both sides of the equation. Although this curve is rather unpleasant, one can easily discuss its general shape, because the two limiting cases

$$\sigma = \frac{Q}{M} = 0 \qquad \text{(nonrelativistic case)}$$
$$\sigma = \frac{Q}{M} = 1 \qquad \text{(ultrarelativistic case)} \tag{7-38}$$

are simple. We shall show that the nonrelativistic case leads to the inscribed circle and the ultrarelativistic case to the inscribed triangle (see Fig. 7-4).

Nonrelativistic case: $\sigma = 0 \rightarrow \rho^2 = 1$. This is the inscribed circle since for $\varphi = \pi$ (direction e in Fig. 7-4) one obtains from (7-32) $\epsilon_3 = 0$, hence the circle touches the sides of the triangle.

Ultrarelativistic case: $\sigma = 1 \rightarrow 2\rho^3 \cos 3\varphi + 3\rho^2 - 1 = 0$. This is the inscribed triangle. That is seen by rewriting this equation by means of $\cos 3\varphi = 4 \cos^3 \varphi - 3 \cos \varphi$, which yields $8(\rho \cos \varphi)^3 + 3\rho^2(1 - 2\rho \cos \varphi) - 1 = 0$, with the solution $\rho \cos \varphi = \frac{1}{2}$; this

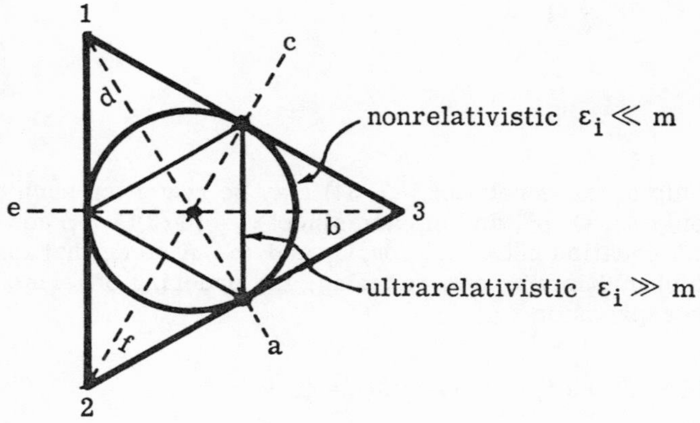

Fig. 7-4 The Dalitz triangle with boundary curves and symmetry lines a, b, c, d, e, f.

represents the vertical side of the inscribed triangle. The two others follow from the symmetry of the figure.

The curves for $0 < \sigma < 1$ lie between the inscribed circle and the inscribed triangle.

D. The Kinematical Situation in Different Regions of the Dalitz Triangle

Let us now discuss to what kinematical situations the different regions of the Dalitz triangle correspond. The symmetry of the figure implies that we need discuss only the region between the lines a and b, say, in Fig. 7-4. [By the way, this symmetry also has the important experimental consequence that the experimental points, which are distributed over the whole region inside the boundary curve, may by repeated reflections all be brought into the region between lines a and b (or some other pair). Thereby one gains practically a factor six in the number of events.]

The center of the triangle corresponds to three equal kinetic energies and hence three equal momenta which include angles of $2\pi/3$. Thus one may picture this situation by saying that the three particles could have flown off from the center of the triangle toward the three corners.

The line center → *a* is a symmetry line on which $\varepsilon_2 = \varepsilon_3 = \frac{1}{2}(Q - \varepsilon_1)$. For $\varepsilon_1 = Q/3$ the center and for $\varepsilon_1 = 0$ the boundary curve is reached. Hence this symmetry line corresponds to $0 \geq \varepsilon_1 \geq Q/3$.

The line center $\rightarrow$ *b* is a symmetry line on which $\varepsilon_1 = \varepsilon_2$, whereas ε_3 varies between Q/3 at the center and the maximum value $\varepsilon_{3,\max}$, which is given by the intersection of b with the boundary.

Exercise: Show that for any of the three kinetic energies

$$\varepsilon_{i,\max} = \frac{1}{2M} Q(M + m) \tag{7-39}$$

The boundary curve corresponds to the equality sign in Eq. (7-33). That means that on the boundary $\cos\theta = \pm 1$; hence $\mathbf{p}_1$ and $\mathbf{p}_2$ have the same or opposite directions and consequently all three momenta are collinear on the boundary curve. Thus we obtain the situation pictured in Fig. 7-5a, b, c.

E. Experimental Applications

Going back to Eq. (7-31), we see that if the situation would be governed by pure kinematics, the distribution of events inside the boundary curve of the Dalitz triangle should be constant. From the foregoing discussion of the kinematical situation corresponding to where an event lies, we may conclude what situations are favored or forbidden by the matrix element when the experimental distribution is not constant. Examples:

A matrix element describing M $\rightarrow$ 3m, where the 3m state has an antisymmetric wave function, will vanish whenever two particles have equal momenta. Therefore near the intersection of b, d, f with the boundary curve (where the situation of Fig. 7-5b is reached) no events should be found.

A matrix element containing cross products of the three-momenta will vanish whenever all three momenta are collinear, i.e., on the boundary curve. In that case the density of experimental points should tend to zero near to the boundary.

It should be stressed again that there might be a considerable background of accidental events (see the discussion on p. 100). This was the case for the ω meson. Another example in which this method has been used is the $\tau \rightarrow 3\pi$ decay (Dalitz, Fabri; see quotations above, p. 100), in which there is no such backtround, because the lifetime of the τ meson is long enough to observe it and see it decay.

How the Dalitz-plot technique was applied to the ω meson is seen in detail in the article by M. L. Stevenson, L. W. Alvarez, B. C. Maglić, and A. H. Rosenfeld, *Phys. Rev.*, **125**, 687 (1962).

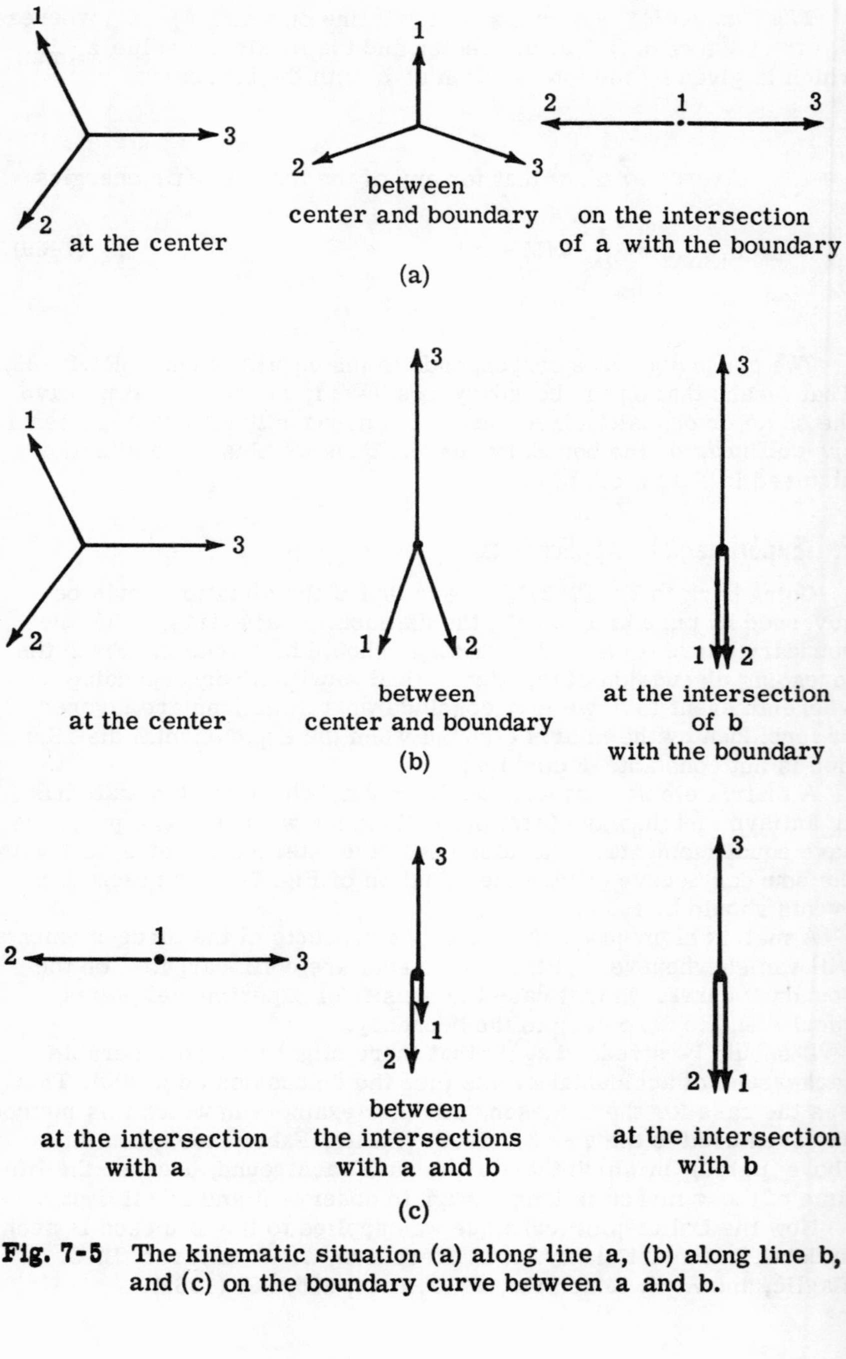

Fig. 7-5 The kinematic situation (a) along line a, (b) along line b, and (c) on the boundary curve between a and b.

7-6 SPECTRA OF DECAY PRODUCTS

A. Statement of the Problem

We consider the following problem, which arises in practice in high-energy physics: In a production process where some particles are created, there may be among them also unstable ones (such as π^0, ρ, η, ω, N^*, etc.) which decay so fast that only their decay products can be observed.

Suppose now that we know somehow what the energy spectrum of the decaying particle is in the over-all center-of-momentum frame of the reaction. What will be the energy spectra of the decay products in the same frame of reference? The answer depends on the angular distribution of the decaying particle and on the angular distribution of the decay products seen from the rest frame of the decaying particle. This is a rather complicated problem. We shall consider a simplified version in which the unstable particle is isotropically distributed in the CM frame and is unpolarized. The latter condition ensures that it decays (seen from its own rest frame) isotropically. Even if these conditions are not strictly fulfilled, the result will give a good approximation to the energy spectra of the decay products, because an energy spectrum is already an average over all angles and therefore the effects of anisotropy will be more or less smeared out.

We shall consider the two-body decay and the three-body decay.

$$m^* \rightarrow m_\ell + m_j$$

$$m^* \rightarrow m_\ell + m_j + m_k$$

In principle, higher decays could also be treated along these lines, but computational difficulties increase rapidly.

It is clear that both decays are determined by kinematics and by the relevant matrix elements. In the two-body decay the matrix element will determine only the lifetime (remember the assumption of m^* being unpolarized) and, since we assume that to be very short, it follows that the energy spectra of the decay products depend only on kinematics. The three-body decay depends, however, explicitly on the matrix element, which determines the energy spectra of the decay products in the m^* rest frame. This is clear from our preceding discussion on the Dalitz plot. Therefore in the three-body decay we have to make assumptions on the matrix element. It is natural to assume again "pure kinematics," namely, a constant matrix element. Deviations of experimental decay spectra may then be due to the nonconstancy of this matrix element (similar to that in the Dalitz plot), or to nonisotropy of the m^* in the CM frame, and in general to both.

Therefore the CM-frame energy spectra of decay products will hardly be used to find out details about the matrix element—the Dalitz plot is much more suited for that. Its main application lies in estimating what the one or the other energy spectrum might be under given experimental conditions (estimates on background, etc.).

The kinematical problem with which we have to work is: We must first calculate the momentum spectra of the decay products in the m^* rest frame. Then, for a given CM momentum of the m^* we must Lorentz-transform these spectra to the CM frame and finally integrate over the m^* spectrum with the condition that the energy of the decay product, seen from the CM frame, lies between η and $\eta + d\eta$. The necessary tools for this are practically all present in the formulas of Chapter 3 and of Sections 7-1 and 7-2.

B. The Two-Body Decay

The situation is shown in Fig. 7-6, where the arrows do not mean momenta but energies; therefore Fig. 7-6 should be taken as an illustration of the notation only, not as a quantitative picture. We use the notation

$m^* \rightarrow m_\ell + m_j$

ε^*, p^* are total energy and magnitude of the three-momentum ($|\mathbf{p}^*|$) of m^* *in the CM frame*

ε_i, p are total energy and magnitude of the three-momentum of either decay product *in the rest frame of m^** ($p_j = p_\ell$!)

η_i is the total energy of either decay product *in the CM frame*

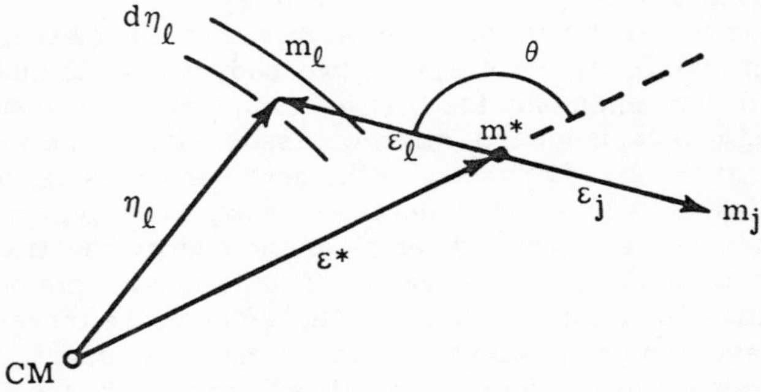

Fig. 7-6 The two-body decay $m^* \rightarrow m_\ell + m_j$.

We first calculate the energy η_ℓ assuming that m^* has the four-momentum $P^* = (\varepsilon^*, \mathbf{p}^*)$ and that m_ℓ has (in the m^* rest frame) the four-momentum $P_\ell = (\varepsilon_\ell, \mathbf{p})$. Then the CM can be considered a fictitious particle, which in the m^* rest frame has the four-momentum $P_{CM} = (\varepsilon^*, -\mathbf{p}^*)$. Therefore in the m^* rest frame we have two four-momenta:

$$\begin{aligned} &\ell \text{ particle:} && P_\ell = (\varepsilon_\ell, \mathbf{p}) \\ &\text{CM ``particle'':} && P_{CM} = (\varepsilon^*, -\mathbf{p}^*) \end{aligned} \tag{7-40}$$

Now Eq. (3-4) states that if P_ℓ and P_{CM} are the four-momenta of any two particles in any Lorentz frame, the energy of particle ℓ, seen from "particle CM," is

$$\eta_\ell = \frac{P_\ell P_{CM}}{m^*} = \frac{1}{m^*}(\varepsilon_\ell \varepsilon^* + pp^*) \tag{7-41}$$

Let θ be the angle between $\mathbf{p}$ and $\mathbf{p}^*$ (see Fig. 7-6); then

$$\eta_\ell = \frac{1}{m^*}\left(\varepsilon_\ell \varepsilon^* + p\sqrt{\varepsilon^{*2} - m^{*2}}\cos\theta\right) \tag{7-42}$$

The momentum p and the energy ε_i of the decay products seen from the m^* rest frame are fixed by the three masses m^*, m_ℓ, m_j and Eq. (3-7) (with an obvious change of notation):

$$\begin{aligned} p^2\left(m^*; m_\ell, m_j\right) &= \frac{\left[m^{*2} - \left(m_\ell + m_j\right)^2\right]\left[m^{*2} - \left(m_\ell - m_j\right)^2\right]}{4m^{*2}} \\ \varepsilon_\ell\left(m^*; m_\ell m_j\right) &= \frac{m^{*2} + \left(m_\ell^2 - m_j^2\right)}{2m^*} \\ \varepsilon_j\left(m^*; m_\ell m_j\right) &= \frac{m^{*2} - \left(m_\ell^2 - m_j^2\right)}{2m^*} \end{aligned} \tag{7-43}$$

The situation is now this:

$w^*(\varepsilon^*)\, d\varepsilon^*$ is the number of unstable particles m^* with energy between ε^* and $\varepsilon^* + d\varepsilon^*$.

$w_\ell(\theta)\, d\cos\theta = \frac{1}{2} d\cos\theta$ is the probability for the ℓ particle going off from m^* in direction θ (the total number, integrated over θ must be 1)

$W_\ell^{(2)}(\eta; m_\ell m_j m^*)\, d\eta$ is the number of ℓ particles having a total CM energy between η and $\eta + d\eta$. This is the spectrum to be calculated. We write normally in a shorter notation $W_\ell^{(2)}(\eta)$ for it.

(In these definitions our assumption of isotropy has been built in. The number $W_\ell^{(2)}(\eta)$ is now found by taking the number of unstable particles with energy ε^*, multiplying it by the probability that the ℓ particle goes in direction θ, and integrating this product over ε^* and θ under the condition that the ℓ particle should have energy η in the CM frame. This condition is ensured by inserting $\delta(\eta - \eta_\ell)$ in the integral, where η_ℓ is taken from (7-42). Hence with $x = \cos\theta$

$$W_\ell^{(2)}(\eta) = \int d\varepsilon^*\, dx\; w^*(\varepsilon^*) \times \tfrac{1}{2}\, \delta\left(\eta - \frac{\varepsilon_\ell \varepsilon^* + xp\sqrt{\varepsilon^{*2} - m^{*2}}}{m^*}\right) \tag{7-44}$$

We see immediately that—as it should be—

$$\int W_\ell^{(2)}(\eta)\, d\eta = \int w^*(\varepsilon^*)\, d\varepsilon^* \tag{7-45}$$

We carry out the integral (7-44) by using

$$\delta(a - bx) = \frac{1}{b}\, \delta\left(x - \frac{a}{b}\right) \tag{7-46}$$

and obtain

$$W_\ell^{(2)}(\eta) = \frac{m^*}{2p} \int d\varepsilon^*\, \frac{w^*(\varepsilon^*)}{\sqrt{\varepsilon^{*2} - m^{*2}}} \times \int_{-1}^{1} dx\; \delta\left(x - \frac{m^*\eta - \varepsilon_\ell \varepsilon^*}{p\sqrt{\varepsilon^{*2} - m^{*2}}}\right) \tag{7-47}$$

The integral over the δ function yields 1 or 0 according to whether or not the argument can become zero for $-1 \le x \le 1$. It gives 1 if

$$-1 \le \frac{m^*\eta - \varepsilon_\ell \varepsilon^*}{p\sqrt{\varepsilon^{*2} - m^{*2}}} \le 1 \tag{7-48}$$

Solving this inequality for ε^* gives two values (quadratic equation) ε_0^* and ε_1^*, between which ε^* must lie to fulfil the inequality. Hence

$$W_{\ell}^{(2)}(\eta; m_{\ell} m_j m^*) = \frac{m^*}{2p(m^*; m_{\ell} m_j)} \times \int_{\varepsilon^*_{\ell_0}}^{\varepsilon^*_{\ell_1}} d\varepsilon^* \frac{w^*(\varepsilon^*)}{\sqrt{\varepsilon^{*2} - m^{*2}}} \tag{7-49}$$

here

$$\varepsilon^*_{\ell \, {}^1_0}(m^*; m_{\ell} m_j) = \frac{m^*}{m_{\ell}^2} \Big[\varepsilon_{\ell}(m^*; m_{\ell} m_j)\, \eta \pm p(m^*; m_{\ell} m_j) \sqrt{\eta^2 - m_{\ell}^2} \Big]$$

his is the solution of the problem stated. In solving the inequality '-48) and in using (7-49), the relations (7-43) which fix ε_{ℓ} and p y means of m^*, m_{ℓ}, and m_j have to be used. $W_j^{(2)}(\eta)$ is found by nterchanging ℓ with j in $\varepsilon^*_{\ell \, {}^1_0}$.

Exercise: Discuss the kinematical meaning of the limits $\varepsilon^*_{\ell \, {}^1_0}$.

. The Three-Body Decay

$$m^* \rightarrow m_{\ell} + m_j + m_k$$

an be reduced to a two-body decay

$$m^* \rightarrow m_{\ell} + M_{jk}$$

here M_{jk} is the rest mass $M_{jk} = \sqrt{(P_j + P_k)^2}$ of the two-particle ystem made up by particles m_j and m_k with four-momenta P_j nd P_k, respectively. The mass M_{jk} is of course not constant; . varies between

$$m_j + m_k \leq M_{jk} \leq m^* - m_{\ell} \tag{7-50}$$

/e have, therefore, the following problem:

We must calculate the probability distribution $P(M_{jk})\, dM_{jk}^2$ for the three-body decay (a special case of the general considerations in Section 7-4).

We must use the two-body formula with a given M_{jk} and integrat it over M_{jk}^2 after multiplication with $P(M_{jk})$. We have therefore,

$$W_\ell^{(3)}(\eta; m_\ell m_j m_k m^*) = \int_{(m_j+m_k)^2}^{(m^*-m_\ell)^2} P(M_{jk}) W_\ell^{(2)}(\eta; m_\ell M_{jk} m^*) \, dM_{jk}^2 \qquad (7\text{-}51)$$

Here the superscripts (2) and (3) denote two-body and three-body decay spectra. We picture the situation again in Fig. 7-7.

We stress here once more that $P(M_{jk})$ depends on the matrix element of the decay and that we have to make an assumption about it. Our assumption will be that the invariant matrix element is constant; i.e., the "pure kinematics of the invariant phase space" determines $P(M_{jk})$. One could also use the "pure kinematics of the noninvariant phase space"—with the same right—but it leads to more complicated formulas.

The only task which remains to make the use of Eq. (7-51) possible is to calculate $P(M_{jk})$ explicitly. For this we use our general formula (7-27), which reads here

$$P(M_{jk}) = \frac{R_2(m^*; M_{jk}, m_\ell) R_2(M_{jk}; m_j, m_k)}{R_3(m^*; m_\ell m_j m_k)} \qquad (7\text{-}52)$$

If we use this formula for $P(M_{jk})$, then by (7-26)

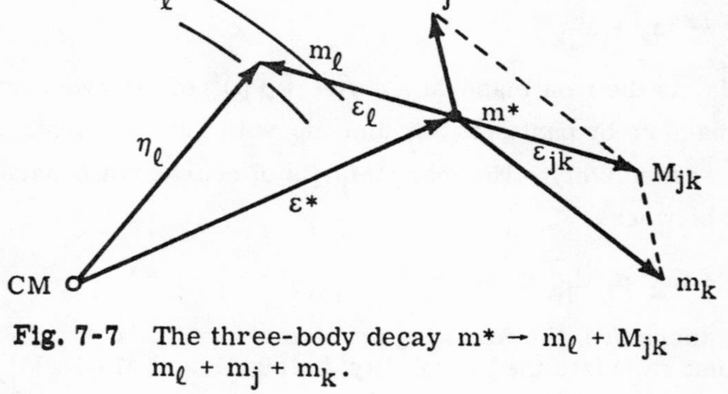

Fig. 7-7 The three-body decay $m^* \to m_\ell + M_{jk} \to m_\ell + m_j + m_k$.

$$\int P(M)\; dM^2 = 1$$

and hence with (7-45)

$$\int W_\ell^{(3)}(\eta; m_\ell m_j m_k)\; d\eta = \int P(M)\; dM^2\; w^*(\varepsilon^*)\; d\varepsilon^*$$
$$= \int w^*(\varepsilon^*)\; d\varepsilon^*$$

which is required by the decay $m^* \to m_\ell + m_j + m_k$ (to each m^* belongs exactly one m_ℓ). Since in the formula for $W_\ell^{(3)}$ numerical integrations will be necessary, there is no point in preserving the normalization (which can always be done numerically at the end). Hence we need not calculate the constant $R_3(m^*, m_\ell m_j m_k)$. The problem is reduced to find an explicit expression for

$$R_2(a;b,c) = \int \frac{d^3 p_b\; d^3 p_c}{2E_b 2E_c}\; \delta(a - \sqrt{p_b^2 + b^2} - \sqrt{p_c^2 + c^2}) \times \delta^3(\mathbf{p}_b + \mathbf{p}_c) \qquad (7\text{-}53)$$

Here we have used the general expression (7-21a) in the rest frame where $P = (a, 0)$. The two particles have masses b and c and the p integrations are performed:

$$d^4p\; \delta(p^2 - m^2) \to \frac{d^3 p}{2E}$$

This formula is easily evaluated. We first integrate over $\mathbf{p}_c$ and obtain

$$R_2(a;b,c) = \int \frac{4\pi p'^2\; dp'}{4\sqrt{p'^2 + b^2}\;\sqrt{p'^2 + c^2}} \times \delta(a - \sqrt{p'^2 + b^2} - \sqrt{p'^2 + c^2}) \qquad (7\text{-}54)$$

The angular integrations give just 4π, since no direction is any longer distinguished. We have put $|\mathbf{p}_b| = |\mathbf{p}_c| = p'$.

Now the δ function can be transformed by means of

$$\delta[f(p')] = \frac{\delta(p' - p)}{\left|\dfrac{df}{dp'}\right|_{p'=p}} \qquad \text{where } f(p) = 0 \qquad (7\text{-}55)$$

Obviously p is the magnitude of the three-momentum of particles b and c if a is the total energy. This p is given by (3-7) or (7-43):

$$p^2 = \frac{[a^2 - (b+c)^2][a^2 - (b-c)^2]}{4a^2} \equiv p^2(a;b,c) \qquad (7\text{-}56)$$

Now with

$$\left|\frac{df}{dp'}\right|_{p'=p} = p\left(\frac{1}{\sqrt{p^2+b^2}} + \frac{1}{\sqrt{p^2+c^2}}\right) = \frac{ap}{\sqrt{p^2+b^2}\,\sqrt{p^2+c^2}}$$

we obtain

$$\begin{aligned} R_2(a;b,c) &= \frac{\pi}{ap}\sqrt{p^2+b^2}\,\sqrt{p^2+c^2} \\ &\quad \times \int \frac{p'^2\,dp'}{\sqrt{p'^2+b^2}\,\sqrt{p'^2+c^2}}\,\delta(p-p') \\ &= \frac{\pi p}{a} \end{aligned}$$

and with (7-56),

$$\begin{aligned} R_2(a;b,c) &= \frac{\pi}{a}p(a;b,c) \\ &= \frac{\pi}{2a^2}\sqrt{[a^2-(b+c)^2][a^2-(b-c)^2]} \end{aligned} \qquad (7\text{-}57)$$

With this result we get for $P(M_{jk})$ [see (7-52)]

$$\begin{aligned} P(M_{jk}) &= \frac{\pi^2}{R_3}\,\frac{1}{m^*}\,\frac{1}{M_{jk}}\,p(m^*;M_{jk},m_\ell) \\ &\quad \times p(M_{jk};m_j m_k) \end{aligned} \qquad (7\text{-}58)$$

We now combine Eqs. (7-51), (7-49), and (7-58) and obtain

$$W_\ell^{(3)}(\eta; m_\ell m_j m_k m^*)$$

$$= \frac{\pi}{R_3} \int dM_{jk}^2 \frac{1}{m^*} \frac{1}{M_{jk}} p(m^*; M_{jk} m_\ell) p(M_{jk}; m_j m_k)$$

$$\times \frac{m^*}{2p(m^*; M_{jk}, m_\ell)} \int_{\varepsilon_0^*}^{\varepsilon_1^*} d\varepsilon^* \frac{w^*(\varepsilon^*)}{\sqrt{\varepsilon^{*2} - m^{*2}}}$$

Hence

$$W_\ell^{(3)}(\eta; m_\ell m_j m_k m^*) = \frac{\pi}{R_3(m^*; m_\ell m_j m_k)} \int_{m_j + m_k}^{m^* - m_\ell} dM \times p(M; m_j m_k) \int_{\varepsilon_{\ell_0}^*}^{\varepsilon_{\ell_1}^*} \frac{d\varepsilon^* \, w^*(\varepsilon^*)}{\sqrt{\varepsilon^{*2} - m^{*2}}} \tag{7-59}$$

where $\varepsilon^*_{\ell_0^1} = \varepsilon^*_{\ell_0^1}(m^*; m_\ell, M)$ is defined below (7-49) and $p(M; m_j m_k)$ in (7-56).

This solves the problem for three-body decay as completely as possible up to the normalization constant $\pi/R_3(m^*; m_\ell m_j m_k)$, which is not important. By interchanging ℓ with j and k one obtains the other two spectra.

8

SHORT CONSIDERATIONS ON RELATIVISTIC NOTATION

So far we have avoided using such terms as "metric tensor," "covariant," and "contravariant" vector components. But sooner or later one may run into trouble with signs if one does not know how to handle these things. They are also used in many books and papers, and in the next paragraph we shall need them explicitly. Since some authors prefer the metric $x^2 = t^2 - \mathbf{x}^2$ and others $x^2 = -t^2 + \mathbf{x}^2$, we shall here confront both notations.

I wish to stress once more the following point: Scalars, vectors, tensor operators, and such things are defined abstractly as physical or geometrical quantities. As soon as a system of coordinates is introduced, these quantities will be represented by components with respect to the coordinate axes. This representation will depend on the choice of the coordinates, whereas the abstract quantities are independent: Their existence logically precedes the existence of coordinates. If in the following we shall find different representations of, e.g., a four-vector by covariant and contravariant components, and, if these representations are different in different metrics, they nevertheless represent one and the same physical quantity.

The "contravariant" components of four-vectors like x or p are defined in any metric:

$$x = (x^0, x^1, x^2, x^3) = (t, \mathbf{x})$$

$$p = (p^0, p^1, p^2, p^3) = (\varepsilon, \mathbf{p}) \qquad (8\text{-}1)$$

They have therefore as components those with "the right sign."

The metric is defined by the "metric tensor" in the two frequently used notations (*we* use that of the right-hand side):

$$g_{\mu\nu} = g^{\mu\nu} = \begin{pmatrix} -1 & & & 0 \\ & 1 & & \\ & & 1 & \\ 0 & & & 1 \end{pmatrix} \quad \Bigg| \quad g_{\mu\nu} = g^{\mu\nu} = \begin{pmatrix} 1 & & & 0 \\ & -1 & & \\ & & -1 & \\ 0 & & & -1 \end{pmatrix} \tag{8-2}$$

Then one obtains the "covariant" components by "lowering" the indices:

$$x_\mu = g_{\mu\nu}\, x^\nu = (x_0, x_1 x_2 x_3) = (-t, \mathbf{x}) \quad \Bigg| \quad x_\mu = g_{\mu\nu}\, x^\nu = (x_0, x_1 x_2 x_3) = (t, -\mathbf{x}) \tag{8-3}$$

Here, and everywhere, the convention is to sum over any double index appearing once up and once down. These sum indices are dummy indices whose names μ, ν, ρ, τ, λ, etc., are irrelevant [see, e.g., (8-6) and (8-7)]. In any tensor (vector) any index can be lowered or raised in this way:

$$\begin{aligned} a_\mu{}^\nu &= a_{\mu\rho}\, g^{\rho\nu} = g_{\mu\rho}\, a^{\rho\nu} \\ a^{\mu\nu} &= g^{\mu\rho}\, a_{\rho\tau}\, g^{\tau\nu} \quad \text{etc.} \end{aligned} \tag{8-4}$$

Applying this rule to the metric tensor itself, it follows that in any metric

$$g_\mu{}^\nu = g_{\mu\tau}\, g^{\tau\nu} = \delta_{\mu\nu} = \begin{pmatrix} 1 & & & 0 \\ & 1 & & \\ & & 1 & \\ 0 & & & 1 \end{pmatrix} \tag{8-5}$$

The scalar product of two four-vectors, e.g., x and p, is defined as the sum over products of covariant with contravariant components:

$$px \equiv p_\mu x^\mu = p^\nu g_{\nu\mu}\, x^\mu = x_\nu\, p^\nu \tag{8-6}$$

In the two metrics this becomes explicitly

$$px = p_\mu x^\mu = p^\rho x_\rho = -\varepsilon t + \mathbf{px} \qquad\Bigg|\qquad px = p_\mu x^\mu = p^\lambda x_\lambda = \varepsilon t - \mathbf{px}$$

$$p^2 = p_\mu p^\mu = -m^2 \qquad\Bigg|\qquad p^2 = p_\mu p^\mu = +m^2 \tag{8-7}$$

Similarly invariants can be formed quite generally, e.g.,

$$aBc \equiv a_\mu B^{\mu\lambda} c_\lambda$$

$$BC \equiv B^{\mu\rho} C_{\rho\mu}$$

The rule is therefore: A quantity is invariant if and only if each index appears twice, once as an upper and once as a lower one.

Care is needed when differentiating. If F is a scalar, dF must be likewise a scalar, i.e., a relativistic invariant. Hence

$$dF = \frac{\partial F}{\partial x_\mu}\, dx_\mu = \frac{\partial F}{\partial x^\nu}\, dx^\nu = \text{invariant} \tag{8-8}$$

Therefore with (8-6) we conclude

$$\frac{\partial F}{\partial x_\mu} \equiv \partial^\mu F \quad \text{are contravariant vector components}$$

$$\frac{\partial F}{\partial x^\mu} \equiv \partial_\mu F \quad \text{are covariant vector components} \tag{8-9}$$

That is: The components of the gradient have the opposite character to the coordinates with respect to which we differentiate. Hence in either metric

$$\frac{\partial}{\partial x^\mu} \equiv \partial_\mu = \left(\frac{\partial}{\partial t}, \frac{\partial}{\partial x}, \frac{\partial}{\partial y}, \frac{\partial}{\partial z}\right) \tag{8-10}$$

whereas the contravariant components of the gradient become

$\frac{\partial}{\partial x_\mu} \equiv \partial^\mu = \left(-\frac{\partial}{\partial t}, \frac{\partial}{\partial x}, \frac{\partial}{\partial y}, \frac{\partial}{\partial z}\right)$	$\frac{\partial}{\partial x_\mu} \equiv \partial^\mu = \left(\frac{\partial}{\partial t}, -\frac{\partial}{\partial x}, -\frac{\partial}{\partial y}, -\frac{\partial}{\partial z}\right)$ (8-11)

The Klein-Gordon operator may be defined as $\Box \equiv \partial_\mu \partial^\mu$ and becomes

$\Box = -\frac{\partial^2}{\partial t^2} + \frac{\partial^2}{\partial x^2} + \frac{\partial^2}{\partial y^2} + \frac{\partial^2}{\partial z^2}$	$\Box = \frac{\partial^2}{\partial t^2} - \frac{\partial^2}{\partial x^2} - \frac{\partial^2}{\partial y^2} - \frac{\partial^2}{\partial z^2}$ (8-17)

A plane wave with positive energy is a physical concept and will be written in either metric

$$\psi_p(x) = \frac{1}{(2\pi)^{3/2}} e^{i(px-\varepsilon t)} \tag{8-13}$$

Therefore the invariant notation will read

$\psi_p(x) = \frac{1}{(2\pi)^{3/2}} e^{+ipx}$	$\psi_p(x) = \frac{1}{(2\pi)^{3/2}} e^{-ipx}$ (8-14)

These plane waves are solutions of the Klein-Gordon equation:

$\Box\psi = \partial_\mu \partial^\mu \psi = -p_\mu p^\mu \psi = m^2 \psi$	$\Box\psi = \partial_\mu \partial^\mu \psi = -p_\mu p^\mu \psi = -m^2 \psi$ (8-15)

Definition: A "covariant" equation means not an equation written in covariant components, but an equation which is consistent in so far as the quantities on both sides transform in the same way: namely, "covariantly." That is to say, both sides must be scalars, vectors, tensors, respectively. In particular, any index which is not a sum index must occur on both sides of the equation and in the same position! A non-covariant equation is wrong (except perhaps in a particular Lorentz frame). Examples:

$a_\mu b^\mu = c$ is correct

$a_\mu b^\mu = D^{\rho\sigma} c_\rho k_\sigma$ is correct

$a_\mu b^\mu c_\lambda = f^\mu$ is wrong

$a_\mu b^\mu c_\lambda = d_\lambda$ is correct

$a_\mu b^\mu c_\lambda = d^\lambda$ is wrong, but $= g_{\lambda\rho}\, d^\rho$ is correct

Problem:

8-1. The tensor of the electromagnetic field is

$$F = \left(F^{\mu\nu}\right) \equiv \begin{pmatrix} 0 & E_x & E_y & E_z \\ -E_x & 0 & H_z & -H_y \\ -E_y & -H_z & 0 & H_x \\ -E_z & H_y & -H_x & 0 \end{pmatrix} \tag{8-16}$$

(a) How do the tensors $F_\mu{}^\nu$, $F^\mu{}_\nu$, $F_{\mu\nu}$ look in our notation ($x^2 = t^2 - \mathbf{x}^2$)?

(b) Write the invariant expression for the trace of a tensor and show that it vanishes for any antisymmetric tensor.

(c) Write down the simplest invariant constructed with F.

(d) Show that the equation

$$\left.\begin{aligned} \frac{\partial F^{\mu\nu}}{\partial x^\nu} &= j^\mu \\ \partial^\rho F^{\mu\nu} + \partial^\nu F^{\rho\mu} + \partial^\mu F^{\nu\rho} &= 0 \end{aligned}\right\} \tag{8-17}$$

give the Maxwell equations $[\, j^\mu = (\rho, \rho\boldsymbol{\beta})]$

Solution to 8-1:

(a) $F_\mu{}^\nu = g_{\mu\rho} F^{\rho\nu}$; $F^\mu{}_\nu = F^{\mu\rho} g_{\rho\nu}$; $F_{\mu\nu} = g_{\mu\rho} F^{\rho\sigma} g_{\sigma\nu}$.

Since g is diagonal, we have always

$$\left| F_\mu{}^\nu \right| = \left| F^\mu{}_\nu \right| = \left| F_{\mu\nu} \right|$$

Since $g_{00} = 1$ and $g_{11} = g_{22} = g_{33} = -1$, we have changes of sign as soon as one index of g is 1 or 2 or 3. Hence

$$F_\mu{}^\nu = \begin{cases} F^{\mu\nu} & \mu = 0 \\ -F^{\mu\nu} & \mu = 1,2,3 \end{cases}$$

$$F^\mu{}_\nu = \begin{cases} F^{\mu\nu} & \nu = 0 \\ -F^{\mu\nu} & \nu = 1,2,3 \end{cases} \qquad (8\text{-}18)$$

Therefore, if one looks at the matrix F, the shaded parts will change sign:

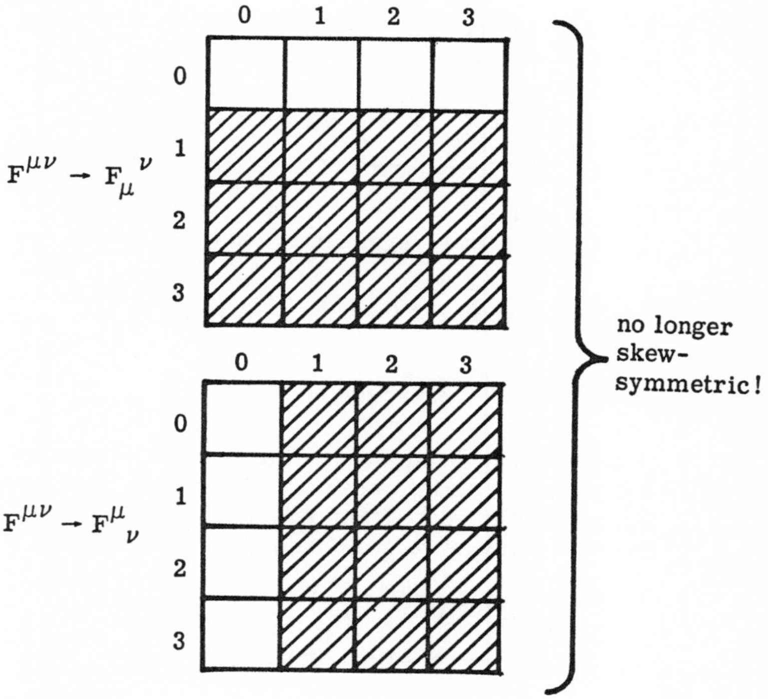

Finally, taking down both indices, both changes occur simultaneously, hence

$F^{\mu\nu} \rightarrow F_{\mu\nu}$

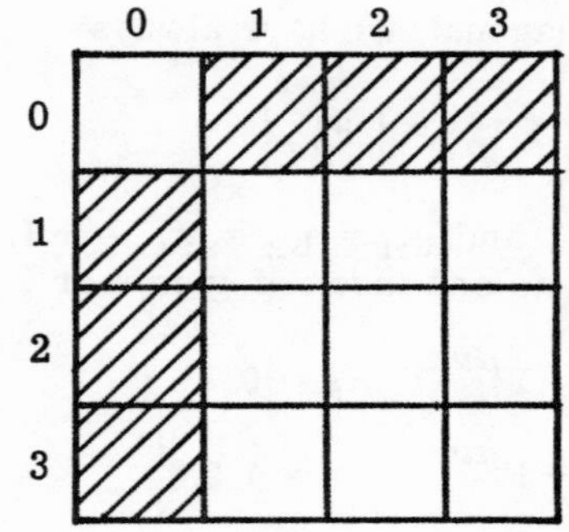

again skew-symmetric

(b) The trace of a tensor $T^{\mu\nu}$ must be written, in order to be invariant:

$$\mathrm{Tr}\ T = T^{\mu}{}_{\mu} = T_{\nu}{}^{\nu} = g_{\nu\mu}\, T^{\mu\nu} \tag{8-19}$$

If $T^{\mu\nu} = -T^{\nu\mu}$, then since the "names" of the sum indices are irrelevant:

$$\underbrace{g_{\nu\mu}\, T^{\mu\nu} = g_{\mu\nu}\, T^{\nu\mu}}_{\nu \text{ and } \mu \text{ interchanged}} \underbrace{= g_{\nu\mu}\, T^{\nu\mu}}_{\text{since } g_{\mu\nu} \text{ is symmetric}} \underbrace{= -g_{\nu\mu}\, T^{\mu\nu}}_{\text{since } T^{\mu\nu} \text{ is antisymmetric}} = 0$$

(c) The simplest invariant, made of F, is

$$F^{\mu\nu}\, F_{\nu\mu} = -F^{\mu\nu}\, F_{\mu\nu}$$

This is—apart from signs—the sum of the squares of all components. As follows from (a), only the E components change sign in going from $F^{\mu\nu}$ to $F_{\mu\nu}$. Since each component occurs twice, we obtain

$$F^{\mu\nu}\, F_{\nu\mu} = -\left(F^{\mu\nu}\, F_{\mu\nu}\right)$$

$$= -2(-\mathbf{E}^2 + \mathbf{H}^2) = 2(\mathbf{E}^2 - \mathbf{H}^2) \tag{8-20}$$

(d) $$\frac{\partial F^{\mu\nu}}{\partial x^{\nu}} = j^{\mu}$$

gives for

$$\mu = 0: \frac{\partial E^k}{\partial x^k} = \rho \qquad \text{or} \qquad \text{div } \mathbf{E} = \rho$$

$$\mu = 1(2;3): -\frac{\partial E_x}{\partial t} + \frac{\partial H_z}{\partial y} - \frac{\partial H_y}{\partial z} = j_x$$

or

$$\text{curl } \mathbf{H} = \mathbf{j} + \frac{\partial \mathbf{E}}{\partial t}$$

$$\partial^{\rho} F^{\mu\nu} + \partial^{\nu} F^{\rho\mu} + \partial^{\mu} F^{\nu\rho} = 0$$

is identically fulfilled as soon as any two indices are equal, this is due to $F^{\mu\nu} = -F^{\nu\mu}$.

Take therefore

$\rho, \mu, \nu = 0,1,2$ etc. [remember (8-11)!]

$$\frac{\partial H_z}{\partial t} - \frac{\partial E_x}{\partial y} + \frac{\partial E_y}{\partial x} = 0 \rightarrow \text{curl } \mathbf{E} = -\frac{\partial \mathbf{H}}{\partial t}$$

$\rho, \mu, \nu = 1,2,3$

$$-\frac{\partial H_x}{\partial x} - \frac{\partial H_y}{\partial y} - \frac{\partial H_z}{\partial z} = 0 \qquad \text{or} \qquad \text{div } \mathbf{H} = 0$$

9

PRECESSION OF THE POLARIZATION OF SPIN ½ PARTICLES MOVING IN AN ELECTROMAGNETIC FIELD†

9-1 THE THREE VECTOR OF POLARIZATION

Although we are leaving with this discussion the pure kinematics, we shall consider this problem here, as it is a nice application of some general techniques, namely, to find the general invariant (or —in this case—covariant) description of a motion or a process or something else by formulating it in a particular reference system by means of the invariants (or covariants) which can be formed with the given four-vectors or tensors. We used this method extensively in Chapters 3 and 6.

Our problem is the following: Suppose a beam of polarized particles is given (the polarization may be described by a polarization vector $\mathbf{s}$, whose length determines the degree of polarization and whose direction coincides with the direction of polarization; see below). Frequently, for technical reasons, this beam has to be guided and deflected by means of lenses and bending fields. What will be the polarization of the beam after such a procedure?

If we consider a particle with spin σ, a measurement of its spin component with respect to a given direction $\mathbf{e}$ (unit vector) will yield one of the $2\sigma + 1$ possible eigenvalues, namely, $m = \sigma, \sigma - 1, \sigma - 2, \ldots, -\sigma$. If we repeat the same experiment very often, i.e., we apply it to a beam, we shall observe a certain frequency distribution $W(\mathbf{e},m)$ of the m values. The average over this distribution is

---

†See, V. Bargmann, L. Michel, and V. L. Telegdi, *Phys. Rev. Lett.*, **2**, 435 (1959).

$$\langle \sigma \cdot \mathbf{e} \rangle = \sum_{m=-\sigma}^{\sigma} W(\mathbf{e},m) \cdot m \tag{9-1}$$

This is the expectation value of the spin component in the direction **e**. The probability distribution W(**e**,m) can be calculated only from quantum theory. The main point, however, is that the expectation value follows a classical equation of motion. This is the consequence of a general theorem by Ehrenfest (see, e.g., L. I. Schiff, *Quantum Mechanics*, 2nd ed., McGraw-Hill, New York, 1955), which states that expectation values of quantum mechanical observables follow classical equations of motion. The expectation value $\langle \sigma \cdot \mathbf{e} \rangle$ may be zero for all choices in the direction **e**; then the beam is unpolarized. (This does not mean that there might not be an "alignment" of spins—but there is nothing left that could be described by a vector polarization.) If this is not the case then there exists a certain direction $\mathbf{e}_0$, in which the expectation value reaches a maximum:

$$\max \langle \sigma \cdot \mathbf{e} \rangle = \langle \sigma \cdot \mathbf{e}_0 \rangle = s \qquad 0 \leq s \leq \sigma \tag{9-2}$$

We then call s the degree of polarization. We may now introduce the polarization vector

$$\mathbf{s} \equiv \mathbf{e}_0 \cdot s \tag{9-3}$$

This vector has an obvious meaning. As it is defined entirely in terms of expectation values, it must follow a classical equation of motion. We know from classical physics that in the rest system of the particles considered this equation of motion is

$$\frac{d\mathbf{s}}{dt} = g\mu_0 \mathbf{s} \times \mathbf{H} \tag{9-4}$$

where $g\mu_0\sigma$ is the magnetic moment of the particles considered. For charged particles, we have

$$g\mu_0\sigma = g\frac{e}{2m}\sigma \tag{9-5}$$

but we shall write $g\mu_0$ in order to cover also the case of neutral particles with magnetic moment (neutron, Λ, Ξ^0, Σ^0). In the Dirac theory $g = 2$, but in quantum electrodynamics corrections are obtained such that $g \neq 2$ for electrons and muons.

9-2 EQUATION OF MOTION OF A "POLARIZATION FOUR-VECTOR"

We shall now generalize this equation into the covariant equation of motion of a polarization four-vector (axial):

$$\left.\begin{aligned} &S \equiv (s_0, \mathbf{s}) \qquad S = (0, \mathbf{s}) \text{ in the rest system} \\ &S^2 = -\mathbf{s}^2 \end{aligned}\right\} \tag{9-6}$$

It is not trivial that such a thing exists, since $\mathbf{s}$ is an axial vector and should be described properly by a skew-symmetric tensor, whose generalization will be a skew-symmetric four-tensor (see, e.g., below, the tensor $F^{\mu\nu}$ of the electromagnetic field). Also, if a polarization four-vector can at all be defined, it is not obvious that its time component should be zero in the particle's rest system. Equation (9-6) is therefore an ansatz and we have to try to see whether it leads to consistent equations.

The rate of change of the polarization at any instant t can depend only on the following quantities:

(a) on the polarization S at that instant t
(b) on the electromagnetic field
(c) on the motion of the particle in that field

The equation of motion of the polarization four-vector, namely, the generalization of Eq. (9-4), will then be of the form

$$\frac{dS}{d\tau} = Z \qquad \tau = \text{proper time of the particle (see pp. 6 and 11)}$$

where Z is a four-vector constructed out of these three quantities. The polarization four-vector S is already defined by Eq. (9-6). The electromagnetic field must be written in its relativistic form as a skew-symmetric tensor [see Problem 8-1]:

$$F^{\mu\nu} = \begin{pmatrix} 0 & E_1 & E_2 & E_3 \\ -E_1 & 0 & H_3 & -H_2 \\ -E_2 & -H_3 & 0 & H_1 \\ -E_3 & H_2 & -H_1 & 0 \end{pmatrix} \begin{aligned} F^{0K} &= E_K \\ F^{ij} &= H_K \end{aligned} \tag{9-7}$$

and the motion of the particle may be described by its four-velocity (see p. 15):

$$V = (\gamma, \gamma\boldsymbol{\beta}) \qquad V = (1,0) \text{ in the rest system} \tag{9-8}$$

We now construct the four-vector Z by generalizing (9-4). We first look for an equation of motion for s_0. We observe first that

$$SV = s_0 v_0 - \mathbf{s v} = 0 \tag{9-9}$$

since this is true in the rest system. Hence

$$\frac{dS}{dt} V = -S \frac{dV}{dt}$$

But in the rest system V = (1,0); therefore

$$\left(\frac{dS}{dt} V\right)_R = \frac{ds_0}{dt} = -S \frac{dV}{dt} \tag{9-10}$$

Thus, in the rest system

$$\left(\frac{dS}{dt}\right)_R \equiv \left(\frac{ds_0}{dt}, \frac{d\mathbf{s}}{dt}\right)_R = \left(-S \frac{dV}{dt}, g\mu_0 \mathbf{s} \times \mathbf{H}\right) = Z_R \tag{9-11}$$

We now express these components by covariant expressions.

(a) All time derivatives will be replaced by derivatives with respect to the proper time. We write a dot:

$$\cdot \text{ means } \frac{d}{d\tau} = \frac{d}{d(t/\gamma)} = \gamma \frac{d}{dt}$$

In the rest system this does not mean any change.

(b) In the rest system $S_R = (0, \mathbf{s}_R)$. Hence, if we use the notation

$$SF \equiv S_\mu F^{\mu\nu} = -F^{\nu\mu} S_\mu = -FS$$

we obtain

$$\mathbf{s}_R \times \mathbf{H} = (SF)_R$$

Therefore

$$(\dot{S})_R = \left(-S\dot{V}, g\mu_0 (SF)_R\right) \equiv Z_R \tag{9-12}$$

(c) We generalize Z_R into a four-vector. We observe that Z_R is linear-homogeneous in S and linear in F. Furthermore, it contains $\dot{V}$. Z, the generalization of Z_R, will therefore be a four-vector: (1) linear homogeneous in S, (2) linear in F.

The only nonconstant four-vectors which can be formed with $S, V, \dot{V}, F$ and which fulfil (1) and (2) are

$$SF \qquad V(S\dot{V}) \qquad V(SFV) \tag{9-13}$$

A product $SF\dot{V}$ is not permitted since $\dot{V}$ = function of F hence $SF\dot{V}$ is not linear in F. Therefore the general form of $\dot{S} = Z$ is

$$\dot{S} = aSF + bV(S\dot{V}) + cV(SFV) \tag{9-14}$$

We now go to the rest system to find a, b, c.

$$(\dot{S})_R = \left\{a(SF)_R^0 + bS\dot{V} + c(SF)_R^0,\ a(SF)_R\right\} \tag{9-15}$$

On the other hand, from (9-12)

$$(\dot{S})_R = \left\{-S\dot{V}, g\mu_0 (SF)_R\right\} \tag{9-16}$$

hence, by comparison, $a = g\mu_0 = -c$; $b = -1$, and therefore with (9-14)

$$\dot{S} = g\mu_0[SF - V(SFV)] - V(S\dot{V}) \tag{9-17}$$

This is the unique generalization of (9-12). Namely, a, b, c have been determined uniquely. A common factor d, say, which in the rest system would reduce to unity, must be equal to one in all systems, since a common factor must be invariant—otherwise it would destroy the four-vector character of $\dot{S}$. An additive term Z', say, cannot exist since in the rest system $Z'_R = (0,0)$, and this remains (0,0) in all Lorentz frames.

This is another example of the rule stated on p. 22, which more generally reads:

> if an equation given in a particular Lorentz system can be written in a manifestly covariant form (that is, both sides have the same transformation property!) which in the particular Lorentz frame reduces to the equation given originally, this covariant form is the unique generalization of the equation given.

Let us return to (9-17).

It should be noted that we tacitly assumed that our particles had:

a constant magnetic moment

no electric moment (of any order) and no higher magnetic moments (quadrupole, etc.)

If these two conditions were violated, our equation in the rest system would already look different. It will then still be possible to define the four-vector S. Complications arise, however, if the particle is also electrically polarizable. Then no such four-vector exists, since only a skew-symmetric tensor in the rest system is sufficient to describe the polarization.

In a homogeneous field one has the equation of motion for a charged particle (that this gives the usual equation of motion, should be checked by the reader).

$$\dot{V} = -\frac{e}{m} FV \tag{9-18}$$

In this case

$$\dot{S} = g\mu_0 SF + \left(\frac{e}{m} - g\mu_0\right) V(SFV) \tag{9-19}$$

where the term with the factor e/m vanishes for neutral particles.

Putting in $g\mu_0 = g(e/2m)$ gives for charged particles

$$\dot{S} = \frac{e}{2m}[gSF - (g - 2)V(SFV)] \tag{9-20}$$

We still have to check the consistency of our formulas:

$$\left.\begin{aligned} S^2 &= -s^2 \\ SV &= 0 \end{aligned}\right\} \tag{9-21}$$

These were the two equations which followed from the definition of the four-vector S. Our equation of motion makes sense only if it does not contradict these equations. Equation (9-21) has the following consequence:

$$S\dot{S} = -(s^2)^{\cdot} = \text{(change of the degree of polarization)}$$

$$\dot{S}V = -S\dot{V}$$

From (9-17) we find

$$\dot{S}V = g\mu_0[SFV - V^2(SFV)] - (S\dot{V})V^2 = -S\dot{V}$$

because $V^2 = 1$. Hence $SV = 0$. Furthermore

$$S\dot{S} = g\mu_0[SFS - SV(SFV)] - SV(S\dot{V}) = 0 = -(s^2)^{\cdot}$$

because $SFS \equiv 0$ (antisymmetry of F!) and $SV = 0$.

This shows that (9-21) is consistent with the equations of motion. We have thus established the existence of a polarization four-vector and found its equation of motion.

9-3 THE POLARIZATION FOUR-VECTOR IN A MOVING FRAME OF REFERENCE

The polarization has an obvious meaning only in the rest system of the polarized particle, whereas the equation of motion has been set up in a covariant form mainly in order to apply it in the lab. system, where the electromagnetic fields are most simply described.

We therefore must study the Lorentz transformation of the polarization between these two systems.

The relevant transformation formula is obtained from p. 9. If we assume in the figure shown there that K′ is the rest system, (R), of the polarized beam, and K the lab. system (L), formula (1-10) gives with $S_R = (0, \mathbf{s}_R)$ replacing $x' = (ct', \mathbf{x}')$ and S_L replacing X:

$$S_L = (s_{oL}, \mathbf{s}_L) = \left(\gamma \boldsymbol{\beta} \mathbf{s}_R,\ \mathbf{s}_R + \boldsymbol{\beta} \frac{\gamma^2}{\gamma + 1} \boldsymbol{\beta} \mathbf{s}_R\right) \tag{9-22}$$

where $\boldsymbol{\beta}$ is the velocity of the polarized beam in the lab. system.

We now may ask: what is $\mathbf{s}_L$? It is a three-vector which indeed has very little to do with what we feel when we hear the word polarization.

Its magnitude depends on $\boldsymbol{\beta}$, since $S^2 = s_0^2 - \mathbf{s}^2 = -s^2$ is invariant. Hence—remember s is the invariant magnitude of polarization—

$$\mathbf{s}_L^2 = s_{oL}^2 + s^2$$

Hence

$$\mathbf{s}_L^2 = s^2[1 + \gamma^2\beta^2 \cos^2(\theta_R)] \tag{9-23}$$

where θ_R is the angle between $\boldsymbol{\beta}$ and the direction of polarization in the rest system. If $\gamma \gg 1$ and $\cos(\theta_R) \neq 0$, $\mathbf{s}_L^2$ increases proportionally to γ^2. For massless particles it becomes ∞. In this case we must use another description (see below).

Its direction depends on $\boldsymbol{\beta}$ as one sees directly in (9-22): If $\gamma \gg 1$, the term $\mathbf{s}_R$ is negligible against the next term which is parallel to $\boldsymbol{\beta}$ if $\boldsymbol{\beta}\mathbf{s}_R > 0$, and antiparallel if it was < 0. That is: When $\beta \to 1$, the polarization three-vector $\mathbf{s}_L$ becomes parallel or antiparallel to $\boldsymbol{\beta}$. The angle is given by

$$\cos^2\theta_L \equiv \cos^2(\mathbf{s}_L\boldsymbol{\beta}) = \frac{(\mathbf{s}_L\boldsymbol{\beta})^2}{\mathbf{s}_L^2\beta^2}$$

This is easily calculated from $SV = \gamma(s_0 - \mathbf{s}\boldsymbol{\beta})_L = 0$; hence with (9-23) and (9-22)

$$\cos^2 \theta_L = \frac{s_{oL}^2}{\beta^2 s_L^2} = \frac{\gamma^2\beta^2 s^2 \cos^2(\theta_R)}{\beta^2 s^2(1+\beta^2\gamma^2 \cos^2(\theta_R))}$$

$$\cos^2 \theta_L = \frac{\gamma^2 \cos^2(\theta_R)}{1+\gamma^2\beta^2 \cos^2(\theta_R)} \qquad (9\text{-}24)$$

This clearly shows that the polarization of a beam should be considered always in the rest system, because the polarization $\mathbf{s}$ of a beam depends on the observer in magnitude and direction.

Introducing the helicity h by helicity = component in the rest system of the polarization in the direction of flight we can write

$$h = s \cos \theta_R = \frac{\mathbf{s}_R \boldsymbol{\beta}}{\beta} = \frac{s_{oL}}{\beta\gamma} = \frac{\mathbf{s}_L \boldsymbol{\beta}}{\beta\gamma} = -sL^\dagger$$

9-4 THE RATE OF CHANGE OF THE DIRECTION OF POLARIZATION

The polarization is completely determined by giving $\mathbf{s}_R$, i.e., by the magnitude (degree of polarization) s and direction of the polarication in the rest system. Our proof of the consistency of the equations of motion with $S^2 = -s^2$ has shown, however, that S^2 is not only invariant, but is even a constant of the motion:

$$\frac{d}{d\tau} S^2 = -\frac{d}{d\tau} s^2 = 0$$

That is, the *degree* of polarization of a beam cannot be changed by passing it through electromagnetic fields whatsoever as long as the inhomogeneities across the beam can be neglected. (Otherwise one must split up the beam into a bundle of sufficiently many smaller beams over whose individual cross sections the fields are constant and calculate the changes of directions of polarization for each one separately. In this case the degree of polarization of the beam as a whole can of course change.)

Therefore, the degree of polarization s is irrelevant for the description of the actual state of polarization and only the directions must be given. That needs two angles. In most cases even one single angle yields the relevant information: the angle between the

---

†See Eqs. (9-27) and (9-28).

polarization in the rest system and the direction of motion. It describes how transversal (or longitudinal) the polarization is.

We shall now give an equation for the rate of change of the angle θ between the polarization $\mathbf{s}_R$ and the direction of motion $\boldsymbol{\beta}$. To this end, we introduce in the lab. system, at the instant $t = t_0$, two unit vectors, one $\boldsymbol{\ell}$ parallel to $\boldsymbol{\beta}$ and the other $\mathbf{n}$ perpendicular to $\boldsymbol{\ell}$ such that $\mathbf{s}_L$ lies in the plane spanned by these two unit vectors (see Fig. 9-1). Then also $\mathbf{s}_R$ lies in the plane spanned by $\mathbf{n}$ (the normal direction) and $\boldsymbol{\ell}$ (the longitudinal direction). Therefore $\boldsymbol{\ell}$ and $\mathbf{n}$ can serve in both reference frames—the lab. and the rest system—and both are defined in an invariant way as far as these two systems are concerned. Clearly

$$\left.\begin{aligned} \boldsymbol{\ell} &= \boldsymbol{\beta}/\beta \\ \mathbf{n}\cdot\boldsymbol{\ell} &= 0 \\ \mathbf{n}^2 &= \boldsymbol{\ell}^2 = 1 \end{aligned}\right\} \tag{9-25}$$

With these unit vectors we can write (9-22)—remember $\theta_R \equiv \measuredangle(\mathbf{s}_R, \boldsymbol{\beta})$—

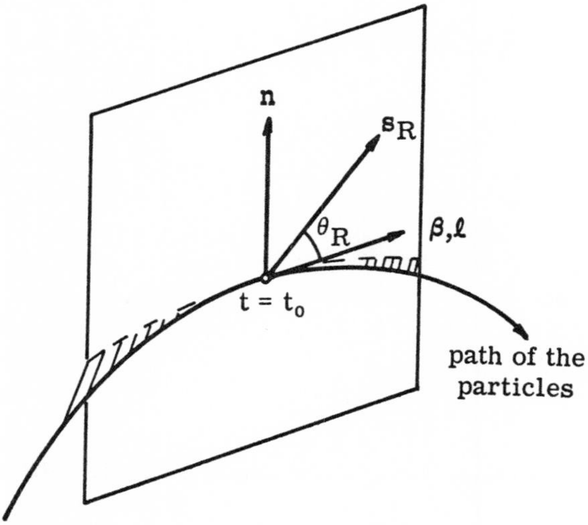

Fig. 9-1 The unit vectors $\mathbf{n}$ and $\boldsymbol{\ell}$ (perspective drawing, $\mathbf{n} \perp \boldsymbol{\ell}$).

$$S_L = (s_{oL}, \mathbf{s}_L)$$

$$= s\left(\beta\gamma \cos\theta_R, \boldsymbol{\ell}\cos\theta_R + \mathbf{n}\sin\theta_R + \boldsymbol{\ell}\frac{\beta^2\gamma^2}{\gamma+1}\cos\theta_R\right)$$

with $\beta^2\gamma^2 = \gamma^2 - 1$ we obtain

$$S_L = s(\beta\gamma \cos\theta_R, \gamma\boldsymbol{\ell}\cos\theta_R + \mathbf{n}\sin\theta_R)$$

$$= s\cos\theta_R(\beta\gamma, \boldsymbol{\ell}\gamma) + s\sin\theta_R(0,\mathbf{n})$$

Introducing the "four-vectors" (we put them in quotation marks, because they behave as four-vectors only with respect to Lorentz transformations in the direction of $\boldsymbol{\beta}$)

$$L \equiv (\beta\gamma, \boldsymbol{\ell}\gamma)$$
$$N \equiv (0,\mathbf{n}) \tag{9-26}$$

we can write†

$$S = sL\cos\theta_R + sN\sin\theta_R \tag{9-27}$$

The particular properties of the "four-vectors" L and N are

$$\left.\begin{aligned} &L^2 = N^2 = -1 \\ &LN = LV = NV = 0 \qquad V = (\gamma, \boldsymbol{\beta}\gamma) \\ &\text{Hence} \\ &L\dot{L} = N\dot{N} = 0 \\ &L\dot{N} = -N\dot{L} \end{aligned}\right\} \tag{9-28}$$

---

†This is also the correct representation in the rest system sinc[e] there we obtain

$$S_R = s(0, \boldsymbol{\ell}\cos\theta_R + \mathbf{n}\sin\theta_R)$$

Indeed, by applying the Lorentz transformation lab. → rest system

/e introduce (9-27) into the equation of motion (9-19) in a homoge-
eous field:

$$\dot{S} = s[\dot{L}\cos\theta_R + \dot{N}\sin\theta_R + \dot{\theta}_R(N\cos\theta_R - L\sin\theta_R)]$$

$$= s\Big[g\mu_0(LF\cos\theta_R + NF\sin\theta_R) - \left(g\mu_0 - \frac{e}{m}\right)V(LFV\cos\theta_R + NFV\sin\theta_R)\Big] \qquad (9\text{-}29)$$

'sing (9-28) we can solve for $\dot{\theta}$ by multiplying by N from the right:

$$\dot{L}N\cos\theta_R - \dot{\theta}_R\cos\theta_R = g\mu_0 LFN\cos\theta_R$$

'he rest annihilates because $NFN \equiv 0$ (F is antisymmetric). Hence

$$\dot{\theta}_R = \dot{L}N - g\mu_0 LFN \qquad (9\text{-}30)$$

nultiplying by L would give the same).

Now the term $\dot{L}N$ is easy to calculate; from (9-26) follows

$$\dot{L}N = -L\dot{N} = \gamma\boldsymbol{\ell}\dot{\mathbf{n}} = -\gamma\mathbf{n}\dot{\boldsymbol{\ell}}$$

n the other hand, writing $V = (\gamma, \boldsymbol{\ell}\beta\gamma)$,

$$N\dot{V} = -\mathbf{n}(\boldsymbol{\ell}(\beta\gamma)^{\cdot} + \beta\gamma\dot{\boldsymbol{\ell}}) = -\beta\gamma\mathbf{n}\dot{\boldsymbol{\ell}}$$

ence

$$\dot{L}N = \frac{1}{\beta}N\dot{V} = -\frac{e}{m}\frac{1}{\beta}NFV$$

, and N are transformed into what they should become, namely

$$L_R = (0, \boldsymbol{\ell}) \qquad \text{and} \qquad N_R = (0, \mathbf{n})$$

'herefore the angle between S and L is the same as between $\mathbf{s}_R$
nd $\boldsymbol{\ell}$.

Introducing this into (9-30) we obtain (AFB = − BFA!)

$$\dot{\theta}_R = \left[\frac{e}{m\beta} V - g\mu_o L\right] FN \tag{9-31}$$

We have with (9-7) and (9-26)

$$FN = F^{\mu\nu} N_\nu = (-\mathbf{E}\mathbf{n}, -\mathbf{n} \times \mathbf{H})$$

$$\frac{e}{m\beta} V - g\mu_o L = \frac{e}{m}\left(\frac{\gamma}{\beta}, \boldsymbol{\ell}\gamma\right) - g\mu_o(\beta\gamma, \boldsymbol{\ell}\gamma)$$

$$= \gamma\left[\frac{e}{m\beta} - \beta g\mu_o, \boldsymbol{\ell}\left(\frac{e}{m} - g\mu_o\right)\right]$$

Inserting this into (9-31) results [with $\dot{\theta}_R = (d\theta_R/d\tau) = \gamma(d\theta_R/dt)$] in

$$\frac{d\theta_R}{dt} = (\mathbf{E}\cdot\mathbf{n})\left(g\mu_o\beta - \frac{e}{m\beta}\right) + \left(g\mu_o - \frac{e}{m}\right)\boldsymbol{\ell}\cdot\mathbf{H}\times\mathbf{n} \tag{9-32}$$

This is valid for any particle with magnetic moment $g\mu_o\sigma$ and charge e. If the charge is ≠ 0, then with $g\mu_o = g(e/2m)$ we obtain

$$\frac{d\theta_R}{dt} = \frac{e}{2m}\left[(\mathbf{E}\cdot\mathbf{n})\frac{(g-2) - g/\gamma^2}{\beta} + (g-2)\boldsymbol{\ell}\cdot\mathbf{H}\times\mathbf{n}\right] \tag{9-33}$$

(Remember: θ_R is the angle between the polarization $\mathbf{s}_R$ and $\boldsymbol{\beta}$ measured in the rest system; **E** and **H** are homogeneous fields in the lab. system.)

Notice that $d\theta_R/dt$ is independent of the degree s of polarization! The case of an electric dipole moment can be described similarly. (See the paper quoted on p. 124.) For inhomogeneous fields one must go back to Eq. (9-17).†

†See also B. H. Good, Jr., *Phys. Rev.*, **125**, 2112 (1962).

It is useful in some cases to combine these equations with (9-29); we therefore list below the various four-vectors appearing on the right-hand side of (9-29), explicitly written in the form of three-vectors:

$$\left.\begin{aligned}
\mathrm{LF} &= -\mathrm{FL} = \gamma(\mathbf{E}\cdot\boldsymbol{\ell},\ \beta\mathbf{E} + \boldsymbol{\ell}\times\mathbf{H}) \\
\mathrm{NF} &= -\mathrm{FN} = (\mathbf{E}\cdot\mathbf{n},\ \mathbf{n}\times\mathbf{H}) \\
\mathrm{VF} &= -\mathrm{FV} = \gamma(\beta\mathbf{E}\cdot\boldsymbol{\ell},\ \mathbf{E} + \beta\boldsymbol{\ell}\times\mathbf{H}) \\
&= \frac{m}{e}\frac{dV}{d\tau} \quad \text{in homogeneous fields} \\
\mathrm{LFV} &= -\mathrm{VFL} = \mathbf{E}\cdot\boldsymbol{\ell} \\
\mathrm{NFV} &= -\mathrm{VFN} = \gamma(\mathbf{E}\cdot\mathbf{n} + \beta\mathbf{n}\cdot\boldsymbol{\ell}\times\mathbf{H})
\end{aligned}\right\} \qquad (9\text{-}34)$$

For the proof of these equations and some examples of applications of Eqs. (9-32) to (9-34) see the Bible, The General Epistle of James 1:22, and Problems 9-1 to 9-4.

Problems:

9-1. Verify Eq. (9-34). The solution is straightforward and follows from the definitions.

9-2. Give a full discussion of the equations of motion for the case of a homogeneous field such that $\mathbf{E}\times\boldsymbol{\ell} = \mathbf{H}\times\boldsymbol{\ell} = 0$.

Solution to 9-2:

(a) We have first to check whether the condition $\mathbf{E}\times\boldsymbol{\ell} = \mathbf{H}\times\boldsymbol{\ell} = 0$ is conserved by the equations of motion of the particle. Indeed, with (9-34) and $\dot{V} = -(e/m)\mathrm{FV}$, we obtain

$$\dot{V} = (\dot{\gamma},\ \dot{\boldsymbol{\ell}}(\beta\gamma) + \boldsymbol{\ell}(\beta\gamma)^{\cdot})$$

$$= \frac{e}{m}\gamma(\beta\mathbf{E}\boldsymbol{\ell},\ \mathbf{E} + \underbrace{\beta\boldsymbol{\ell}\times\mathbf{H}}_{=0 \quad \text{at a time } t_0})$$

Writing $\mathbf{E} = \boldsymbol{\ell} E$ we see that $\dot{\boldsymbol{\ell}} = 0$. All higher derivatives of $\boldsymbol{\ell}$ also vanish. Hence $\boldsymbol{\ell}$ is constant and the condition $\boldsymbol{\ell} \times \mathbf{E} = \boldsymbol{\ell} \times \mathbf{H} = 0$ is conserved.

(b) Now (9-32) tells us immediately

$$\frac{d\theta_R}{dt} = 0$$

(c) $\dot{S}$ however is not zero. We take (9-29) with $\dot{\theta} = 0$:

$$\dot{S} = s(\dot{L} \cos\theta_R + \dot{N} \sin\theta_R)$$

$$= s\left(\gamma \frac{e}{m} E \cos\theta_R,\ \beta\gamma \frac{e}{m} E\boldsymbol{\ell} \cos\theta_R + g\mu_0 \mathbf{n} \times \mathbf{H} \sin\theta_R\right)$$

Here (9-34) was used to write down explicitly the right-hand side of Eq. (9-29). Comparing coefficients gives

$$\dot{L} = \frac{e}{m} E(\gamma, \boldsymbol{\beta}\gamma) = \frac{e}{m} EV$$

which gives $V\dot{L} = (e/m)E = -L\dot{V}$, as it should be, and

$$\dot{N} = g\mu_0 \mathbf{n} \times \mathbf{H}$$

These equations state that L changes because the particle is accelerated and that N precesses in a left screw and with constant angular frequency around **H**:

$$\frac{dN}{dt} = \frac{dn}{dt} = \frac{1}{\gamma}\dot{N} = \frac{1}{\gamma}\dot{n} = \frac{g\mu_0}{\gamma} \mathbf{n} \times \mathbf{H} \qquad \left|\frac{dn}{dt}\right| = \omega = \frac{g\mu_0 H}{\gamma}$$

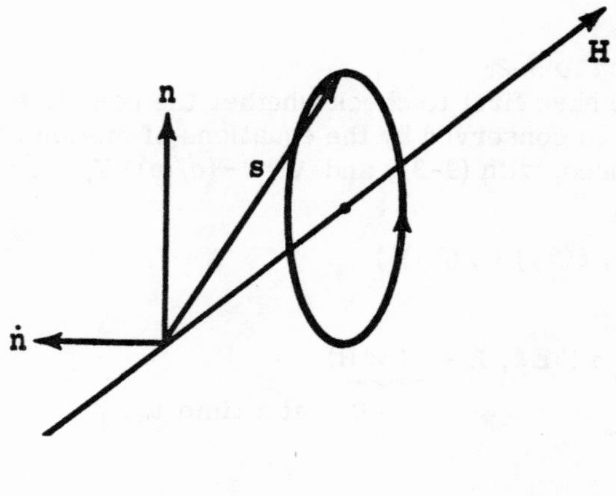

Problem:

9-3. Consider the case $\mathbf{E} = 0$; $H(\mathbf{n} \times \boldsymbol{\ell}) = \mathbf{H}$ in the same way as in the previous problem.

Solution to 9-3:

(a) We first check whether these conditions are conserved, using again the equations of motion of the particle (9-34):

$$\dot{V} = [\dot{\gamma}, \dot{\boldsymbol{\ell}}\beta\gamma + \boldsymbol{\ell}(\beta\gamma)^{\cdot}] = \frac{e}{m}\gamma(0, \beta \mathbf{n} H)$$

It follows that

$$\dot{\boldsymbol{\ell}} = \frac{eH}{m}\mathbf{n}$$

which means that $\boldsymbol{\ell}$ and $\mathbf{n}$ rotate with angular frequency

$$\left|\frac{d\boldsymbol{\ell}}{dt}\right| = \frac{eH}{m\gamma} = \omega_0$$

in a left-screw around $\mathbf{H}$.

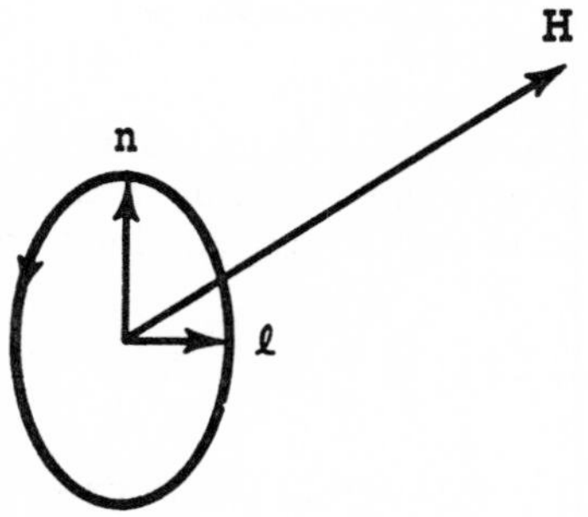

Therefore the condition is conserved. This is the well-known behavior of a charge moving in a constant magnetic field: It goes on circles with angular frequency ω_0 (Larmor frequency).

(b) The equation of motion (9-32) for θ_R now gives

$$\frac{d\theta_R}{dt} = \left(g\mu_0 - \frac{e}{m}\right)H = \frac{eH}{m}\left(\frac{g}{2} - 1\right)$$

That is, the angle between the direction of motion and the polarization increases (or decreases) with constant rate if $g \neq 2$. Note that this is independent of the velocity of the particles! The particles move on a circle and turn around once in the time $T = 2\pi/\omega_0 = 2\pi(m\gamma/eH)$. Therefore

$$\Delta\theta_R = \theta_R(T) - \theta_R(0) = T\,\frac{d\theta_R}{dt} = 2\pi\gamma\left(\frac{g}{2} - 1\right)$$

Since after one turn $\boldsymbol{\ell}$ has its old position, this $\Delta\theta_R$ is the change of the direction of polarization per turn.

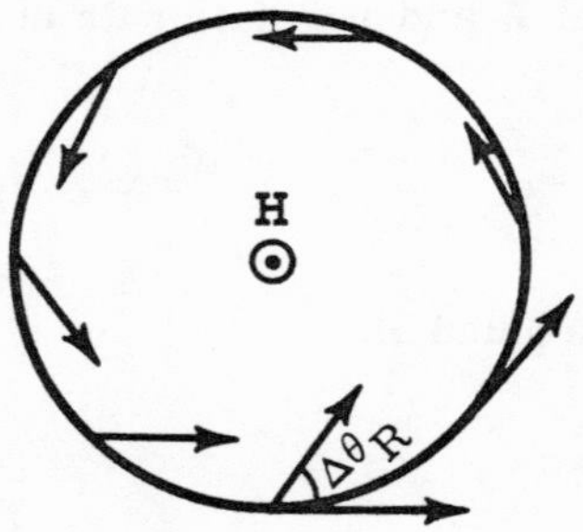

See the figure above ($g > 2$ was assumed). This fact has been used to measure the g factor of the μ. Further examples are found in the reference given on p. 124.

Problem:

9-4. Regarding Eq. (9-32) in the case of a fictitious particle with spin and with $e \neq 0$, but without magnetic moment ($g = 0$), one sees that

$$\frac{d\theta_R}{dt} = -\frac{e}{m}\left[\frac{En}{\beta} + \boldsymbol{\ell}\cdot\mathbf{H}\times\mathbf{n}\right]$$

Physical intuition tells us, however, that the polarization should not change if there is no magnetic moment. Show that there is no contradiction.

Solution to 9-4:

Since θ_R is the angle between the polarization and the direction of motion and since we expect that the polarization $\mathbf{s}_R$ = const., we presume that $d\theta_R/dt$ describes the change of the direction of motion with respect to any fixed direction. We calculate everything in the lab. system.

(a) From (9-34) we have ($' \equiv d/dt = d/\gamma\, d\tau$)

$$\dot{V} = \gamma V' = \frac{e\gamma}{m}(\beta \mathbf{E}\boldsymbol{\ell}, \mathbf{E} + \beta\boldsymbol{\ell} \times \mathbf{H})$$

$$= \gamma(\gamma', \beta\gamma\boldsymbol{\ell}' + \boldsymbol{\ell}(\beta\gamma)')$$

Hence, comparing time components

$$\gamma' = \frac{e}{m}\mathbf{E}\boldsymbol{\ell}\beta$$

Further

$$(\beta\gamma)' = \frac{\gamma'}{\beta} = \frac{e}{m}\mathbf{E}\boldsymbol{\ell}$$

Therefore, comparing space components

$$\frac{e}{m}(\mathbf{E} + \beta\boldsymbol{\ell} \times \mathbf{H}) = \beta\gamma\boldsymbol{\ell}' + \frac{e}{m}\boldsymbol{\ell}(\mathbf{E}\boldsymbol{\ell})$$

$$\boldsymbol{\ell}' = \frac{e}{m\beta\gamma}[\mathbf{E} - \boldsymbol{\ell}(\mathbf{E}\boldsymbol{\ell}) + \beta\boldsymbol{\ell} \times \mathbf{H}]$$

(b) At a given instant t_0 we take in the lab. system a constant four-vector $A = S(t_0)$. Then

$$A = L\cos\theta + N\sin\theta \qquad \theta(t_0) = \theta_R$$

$$A' = L'\cos\theta + N'\sin\theta + \theta'(N\cos\theta - L\sin\theta) = 0$$

Therefore by multiplication by N [see Eqs. (9-26) and (9-28)]

$$\theta' = NL' = -\gamma \mathbf{n}\boldsymbol{\ell}'$$

Taking the $\boldsymbol{\ell}'$ just calculated, we find

$$\theta' = -\frac{e}{m}\left[\frac{\mathbf{En}}{\beta} + \boldsymbol{\ell}\cdot\mathbf{H}\times\mathbf{n}\right]$$

which coincides with $d\theta_R/dt$, as stated in the problem.

9-5 THE CASE OF MASS ZERO

Our polarization four-vector

$$S^\mu = \left(\gamma\boldsymbol{\beta}\mathbf{s}_R,\ \mathbf{s}_R + \boldsymbol{\beta}\frac{\gamma^2}{\gamma+1}\boldsymbol{\beta}\mathbf{s}_R\right)$$

does not work, since $\gamma \to \infty$ and $\mathbf{s}_R$ is meaningless. On the other hand, on p. 132 I said that "polarization" is defined only in the rest system. Clearly, our whole concept fails to apply to particles with mass zero. And yet particles with mass zero and spin $\neq 0$ exist.

We may solve the problem by analogy with the four-velocity: $V^\mu = (\gamma, \boldsymbol{\beta}\gamma)$ is also diverging if we consider $m \to 0$. There exists, however, another four-vector, which is proportional to V and does not become meaningless for $m \to 0$, namely, the four-momentum $P = mV = (m\gamma, m\boldsymbol{\beta}\gamma) = (\varepsilon, \mathbf{p})$.

Let us multiply S by m and consider the four-vector

$$W^\mu = mS^\mu = \left(m\gamma\boldsymbol{\beta}\mathbf{s}_R,\ m\mathbf{s}_R + \boldsymbol{\beta}\frac{m\gamma^2}{\gamma+1}\boldsymbol{\beta}\mathbf{s}_R\right) \qquad (9\text{-}35)$$

Let us forget about the meaning of $\mathbf{s}_R$ and look at $|\mathbf{s}_R| \cos(\boldsymbol{\beta}\mathbf{s}_R)$ as a constant s. Then

$$W^\mu = \left(m\gamma\beta s,\ m\mathbf{s}_R + \boldsymbol{\beta}\frac{m\gamma^2}{\gamma+1}\beta s\right)$$

This W^μ transforms as a four-vector, no matter what origin the constant s has: If we give this expression to somebody and tell him that this were m times the polarization four-vector of a particle with four-momentum P, then he is able to tell us how this four-vector will look in any other Lorentz system. This is sufficient. As long as $m \neq 0$, he can even transform to the rest system and discover the physical significance of the constant s.

But now we allow the mass to go to zero. Then, with $\gamma \to \infty$, $\boldsymbol{\beta} \to \boldsymbol{\ell}$,

$$W^{\mu}(m \to 0) = s(\varepsilon, \boldsymbol{\ell}\varepsilon) = sP^{\mu}(m = 0)$$

We may again call $|s|$ the degree of polarization and find

$$\left.\begin{aligned} m = 0: \quad & W^{\mu} = sP^{\mu} \\ & \mathbf{s} = s\boldsymbol{\ell} \\ & W^{\mu}W_{\mu} = W^{\mu}P_{\mu} = P^{\mu}P_{\mu} = 0 \end{aligned}\right\} \tag{9-36}$$

That is, since W^{μ} and P^{μ} are four-vectors, s must be an invariant. The direction of polarization is always parallel $(s > 0)$ or antiparallel $(s < 0)$ to the direction of motion and the magnitude s is the same in all Lorentz frames: the helicity is always $\pm s$. There is therefore no need for an equation of motion of the polarization.

Our representation of the polarization of massless particles used here is different from that for polarized light by means of the Stokes parameters (see the lecture of R. Hagedorn, "Density Matrix," *CERN*, 58-7), but it is also applicable to light quanta.

9-6 THE RELATION OF THE POLARIZATION FOUR-VECTOR TO THE ANGULAR-MOMENTUM TENSOR

A. Intrinsic and Orbital Angular Momentum of a System of Spinless Particles

We defined S as the expectation value of the spin of a beam. It therefore follows classical equations of motion. This suggests to try to establish a connection between S and the angular momentum of a classical system. Corresponding relations will then exist between the operators.

We consider a closed system of N spinless classical mass points with coordinates and momenta

$$x_i^\mu = (t, \mathbf{x}_i) \qquad i = 1 \cdots N$$
$$p_i^\mu = (\varepsilon_i, \mathbf{p}_i)$$

The angular momentum of the system is the skew-symmetric tensor

$$M^{\mu\nu} = \sum_i x_i^\mu p_i^\nu - x_i^\nu p_i^\mu \tag{9-37}$$

The time components are†

$$M^{ok} = t \sum p^k - \sum x^k \varepsilon \tag{9-38}$$

Introducing the total four-momentum

$$P = \sum p_i = (\Sigma\, \varepsilon, \Sigma\, \mathbf{p}) \tag{9-39}$$

and going to the rest system ($\mathbf{P} = 0$), we obtain

$$\left(M^{ok}\right)_R = -\left(\sum x^k \varepsilon\right)_R$$

From angular-momentum conservation, it follows that this quantity is constant in time. We define now in R the four-vector (with constant space components!)

$$\left(X^\mu\right)_R = \left(t, \frac{1}{\Sigma\, \varepsilon_i} \sum \mathbf{x}_i\, \varepsilon_i\right)_R$$

Since R is defined invariantly [starting from any Lorentz system, the condition $\Sigma \mathbf{p} = 0$ leads always to the same system R (up to a space rotation and translation)], the four-vector $(X^\mu)_R$ is defined invariantly and may then be transformed to any Lorentz system. We call this general X the center of gravity (CG):

---

†Notation: Greek indices $0 \cdots 3$; Latin indices $1 \cdots 3$. The indices i labeling the mass points will be suppressed wherever possible.

$$X^\mu = L(X^\mu)_R = L\left(t, \frac{\Sigma\, x\varepsilon}{\Sigma\, \varepsilon}\right)_R \tag{9-40}$$

ie notation means that $(X^\mu)_R$ has to be Lorentz-transformed to tain X^μ. This X^μ is different from what one would obtain by orentz transforming each x_i^μ and p_i^μ and constructing $(t, \Sigma\, x\varepsilon/\Sigma\, \varepsilon)$ the new Lorentz frame. Therefore we had to define X^μ in this omplicated way to make sure that it is a four-vector. The word center of gravity" is chosen because for nonrelativistic particles e have

$$\left(\frac{\Sigma\, x\varepsilon}{\Sigma\, \varepsilon}\right)_R \to \frac{\Sigma\, xm}{\Sigma\, m}$$

ow in the rest system R (where $\mathbf{P} = 0$) we may introduce new co- dinates $x_{i,CG}^\mu$ by measuring all distances from the center of avity $(X^\mu)_R$ (see Fig. 9-2):

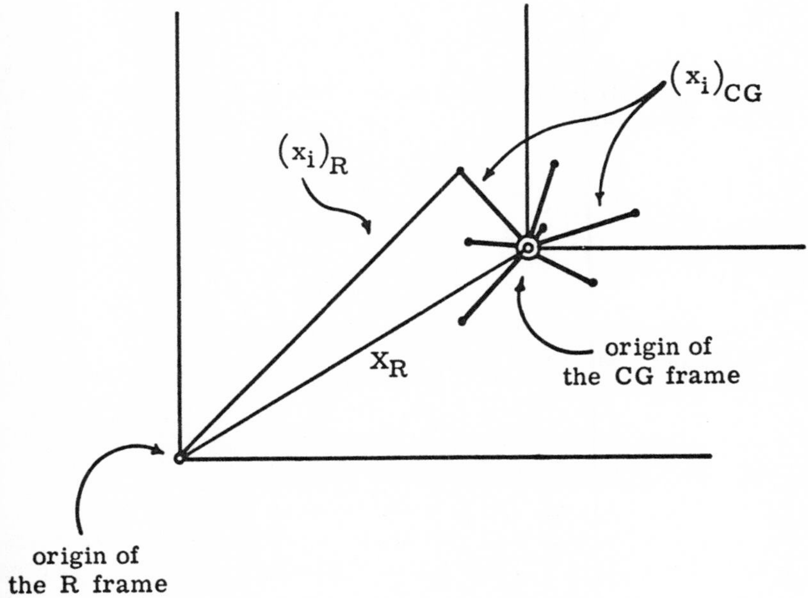

Fig. 9-2 The center of gravity.

$$(x_i)_R = X_R + (x_i)_{CG} \qquad (9\text{-}41)$$

Note that the $(x_i)_{CG}$ have the time components zero. The moment remain unchanged. Then the angular momentum tensor becomes in R

$$\begin{aligned}(M^{\mu\nu})_R &= \Sigma\,(x^\mu p^\nu - x^\nu p^\mu)_R \\ &= \Sigma\,(x^\mu p^\nu - x^\nu p^\mu)_{CG} \\ &\quad + (X^\mu P^\nu - X^\nu P^\mu)_R \end{aligned} \qquad (9\text{-}42)$$

and the general $M^{\mu\nu}$ in any Lorentz system is found by a suitable Lorentz transformation. This $(M^{\mu\nu})_R$ has remarkable properties If we imagine the origin in R shifted to X_R, the term $X^\mu P^\nu - X^\nu P^\mu$ vanishes since then $\mathbf{P} = 0$ and $\mathbf{X} = 0$. Therefore the term

$$\Sigma\,(x^\mu p^\nu - x^\nu p^\mu)_{CG}$$

represents the intrinsic angular momentum of the system. It has no time components:

$$\Sigma\,(x^0 p^k - x^k \varepsilon)_{CG} = 0$$

since $\Sigma\, p^k = 0$ and $\Sigma\, x^k \varepsilon = X^k \Sigma\, \varepsilon = 0$.

We define now

$$\begin{aligned}\Sigma\,(x^\mu p^\nu - x^\nu p^\mu)_{CG} &\equiv (S^{\mu\nu})_R \\ (X^\mu P^\nu - X^\nu P^\mu)_R &\equiv (L^{\mu\nu})_R\end{aligned} \qquad (9\text{-}43)$$

Only the three components of $(S^{\mu\nu})_R$ are different from zero: $(S^{23}, S^{31}, S^{12})_R$, and they can be considered as the three components of an axial vector $\mathbf{s}_R$. We shall come back to this later.

Now by an arbitrary Lorentz transformation,

$$M^{\mu\nu} = S^{\mu\nu} + L^{\mu\nu} = S^{\mu\nu} + X^\mu P^\nu - X^\nu P^\mu \qquad (9\text{-}44)$$

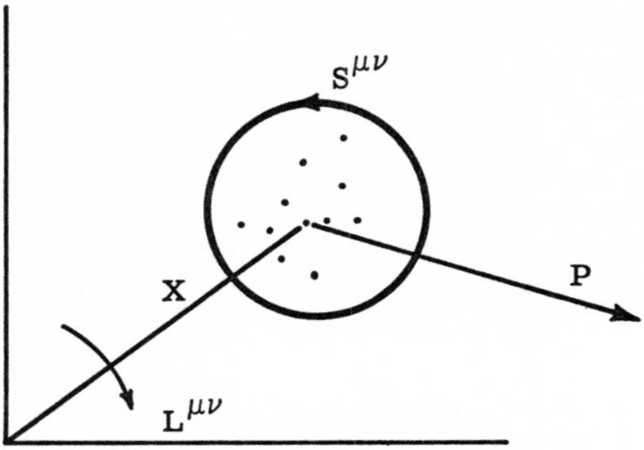

Fig. 9-3 Intrinsic and orbital angular momentum.

'e have thus separated in a covariant way the orbital part $L^{\mu\nu}$ 'om the intrinsic part $S^{\mu\nu}$ of the total angular momentum $M^{\mu\nu}$;ee Fig. 9-3). We note one important covariant property of $^{\mu\nu}$, namely,

$$S^{\mu\nu}P_\nu = 0 \tag{9-45}$$

his is true in the rest system R, because there $S^{ok} = 0$ and $\mathbf{P} = 0$. ut if the four-vector $S^{\mu\nu}P_\nu$ is zero in one system, it is zero in .l Lorentz systems (all its components vanish).

. The Relation between the Intrinsic Angular-Momentum Tensor and the Polarization Four-Vector

Equation (9-45) is an implicit definition of $S^{\mu\nu}$, but it cannot erve to find $S^{\mu\nu}$ once $M^{\mu\nu}$ is given. On the other hand, since we ere able to define $S^{\mu\nu}$ in a covariant way (although in a rather omplicated description involving words), we also should be able define it by means of a covariant formula (remember the re- arks on p. 22).

Roughly speaking, we shall do something like this: by multiply- ıg $M^{\mu\nu}$ by P_ν we obtain

$$M^{\mu\nu}P_\nu = L^{\mu\nu}P_\nu$$

since

$$S^{\mu\nu} P_\nu = 0$$

If we could undo the multiplication by P_ν, we would have projected out the $L^{\mu\nu}$ part and then $S^{\mu\nu} = M^{\mu\nu} - L^{\mu\nu}$. Actually it is not quite so simple but we can do it in two steps:

(a) We introduce the completely antisymmetric tensor $\varepsilon_{\mu\nu\rho\sigma}$ of rank four:

$$\varepsilon_{\mu\nu\rho\sigma} = \begin{cases} +1 & \text{if } (\mu\nu\rho\sigma) \text{ is even} \\ -1 & \text{if } (\mu\nu\rho\sigma) \text{ is odd} \end{cases} \tag{9-46}$$

"Even" and "odd" mean that $(\mu\nu\rho\sigma)$ is obtained from (0123) by an even or odd number of transpositions, respectively. Consequently, $\varepsilon_{\mu\nu\rho\sigma}$ is zero if any two indices are equal; $\varepsilon_{\mu\nu\rho\sigma} = -\varepsilon_{\nu\rho\sigma\mu}$ (cyclic permutation). Furthermore, raising or lowering one index (by means $g^{\mu\nu}$) changes the sign if that index was 1,2,3; it does not change the sign if that index was 0.

With this $\varepsilon_{\mu\nu\rho\sigma}$ we define the (pseudo-) four-vectors

$$\begin{aligned} W^\mu &= \tfrac{1}{2}\varepsilon^\mu{}_{\nu\rho\sigma} P^\nu M^{\rho\sigma} = \tfrac{1}{2}\varepsilon^\mu{}_{\nu\rho\sigma} P^\nu S^{\rho\sigma} \\ S^\mu &= \frac{1}{m} W^\mu \qquad m \equiv \sqrt{P^2} \end{aligned} \tag{9-47}$$

The second member of the first equation is true, since the orbital part drops out:

$$\varepsilon^\mu{}_{\nu\rho\sigma} P^\nu \left(X^\rho P^\sigma - X^\sigma P^\rho\right) = 0$$

each term vanishes because of the antisymmetry of ε. The physical significance of W^μ is easily found by going to the rest system where $\mathbf{P} = 0$ and $P^0 = m$:

$$(W^0)_R = \tfrac{1}{2}\varepsilon^0{}_{0\rho\sigma} \left(P^0 S^{\rho\sigma}\right)_R = 0$$

because of the antisymmetry of ε.

$$(W^1)_R = (\tfrac{1}{2}\varepsilon^1{}_{023}P^0S^{23} + \tfrac{1}{2}\varepsilon^1{}_{032}P^0S^{32})_R = m(S^{23})_R$$

Similarly,

$$(W^2)_R = m(S^{31})_R \qquad \text{and} \qquad (W^3)_R = m(S^{12})_R$$

Hence

$$(W^\mu)_R = m(0,S^{23},S^{31},S^{12})_R = m(S^\mu)_R \equiv (0,\mathbf{s}_R) \tag{9-48}$$

We see that in the rest frame W^μ reduces to a three-vector $m\mathbf{s}_R$, whose three components are equal to the three nonvanishing components of (m times) the intrinsic angular-momentum tensor. In this particular system R the intrinsic angular momentum can therefore be described by a (pseudo- or axial) vector $\mathbf{s}_R$ (similarly as the magnetic field can be described by an axial vector). Now, if we go to an arbitrary frame, W^μ transforms as a four-vector and $S^{\mu\nu}$ as a tensor. They are different things indeed, but in R "they touch each other" in the sense of Eq. (9-48).

If we allow, in our thoughts, our system of N spinless particles to shrink to almost one point, so that we no longer can distinguish its N constituents, it becomes what we would call a particle with mass m, momentum P, and intrinsic angular momentum or spin $S^{\mu\nu}$ (the square of the magnitude of the spin would be the invariant $s^2 = |\mathbf{s}_R|^2 = -S^\mu S_\mu$). It should be stressed, however, that we are playing here with an analogy only: By this kind of argument we never would obtain half-integer values of s, not even by invoking quantum mechanics. But quantum mechanics provide us with an additional kind of angular momentum, namely, the spin, which, as a kinematical quantity, behaves indeed as our $S^{\mu\nu}$; in particular it holds that $S^{\mu\nu}P_\nu = 0$ [see the remark below Eq. (9-68)].

But it can no longer be considered as coming from the bodily rotation of N mass points clustered together. Therefore, from now on we shall consider $S^{\mu\nu}$ as a really new thing which cannot be understood from analyzing the "structure and rotation" of the particle. If, e.g., one considers an electron as a rotating sphere of uniform mass distribution, its moment of inertia is $T = \frac{2}{5}mr^2$, its angular momentum is $s = \frac{1}{2}\hbar = \omega \cdot T$, where $\omega = v/r$ is its angular velocity and v is the velocity at its equator. Then

$v = (r/2)(\hbar/T) = \frac{5}{4}(\hbar/mr)$; putting $r = e^2/mc^2$ one finds $v/c = \frac{5}{4}(\hbar c/e^2) = \frac{5}{4} \times 137 \gg c$. This contradicts relativity!

Clearly W^μ and S^μ are identical with our previously defined quantities because they are the same in the rest frame. However, so far this is only true as long as we deal with one single spinning particle. We shall remove partly this restriction later on.

(b) We see that in Eq. (9-47) the intrinsic part $S^{\mu\nu}$ is projected out of $M^{\mu\nu}$. And now this equation can in fact be solved for $S^{\mu\nu}$ in the following way:

$$S^{\mu\nu} = \frac{1}{m^2}\,\varepsilon^{\mu\nu}{}_{\alpha\beta}\,P^\alpha W^\beta \tag{9-49}$$

which is the inverse of (9-47). Since this is a covariant equation, it suffices to prove it in the rest system ($\mathbf{P} = 0$; $P^0 = m$). Indeed:

$$(S^{12})_R = \frac{1}{m^2}\,\varepsilon^{12}{}_{03}(P^0 W^3)_R = \frac{1}{m^2}\,\varepsilon^{12}{}_{03}\, m \cdot m (S^{12})_R = (S^{12})_R$$

$$(S^{ok})_R = \frac{1}{m^2}\,\varepsilon^{ok}{}_{oi}(P^0 W^i)_R = 0 \qquad \text{because} \qquad \varepsilon^{ok}{}_{oi} = 0$$

And now we only need to introduce (9-47):

$$W^\beta = \tfrac{1}{2}\varepsilon^\beta{}_{\lambda\rho\sigma}\,P^\lambda M^{\rho\sigma}$$

into (9-49) to obtain

$$S^{\mu\nu} = \left[\frac{1}{2m^2}\,\varepsilon^{\mu\nu}{}_{\alpha\beta}\,\varepsilon^\beta{}_{\lambda\rho\sigma}\,P^\alpha P^\lambda\right] M^{\rho\sigma} \equiv \Sigma^{\mu\nu}{}_{\rho\sigma}\,M^{\rho\sigma}$$

$$\Sigma^{\mu\nu}{}_{\rho\sigma} = \frac{1}{2m^2}\,\varepsilon^{\mu\nu}{}_{\alpha\beta}\,\varepsilon^\beta{}_{\lambda\rho\sigma}\,P^\alpha P^\lambda = \varepsilon^{\mu\nu}{}_{\alpha\beta}\left(\frac{P^\beta P_\lambda}{2m^2}\right)\varepsilon^{\lambda\alpha}{}_{\rho\sigma} \tag{9-50}$$

where $\Sigma^{\mu\nu}{}_{\rho\sigma}$ is the desired projection operator. Indeed

$$S^{\mu\nu} P_\nu = 0$$

since

$$\varepsilon^{\mu\nu}{}_{\alpha\beta}\,\varepsilon^{\beta}{}_{\lambda\rho\sigma}\,P^{\alpha}P^{\lambda}P_{\nu} = 0$$

because of the asymmetry of ε.

We have accomplished two things: We have split the angular momentum tensor $M^{\mu\nu}$ for one spinning particle (or else for a system of spinless particles) in a covariant way into the intrinsic part $S^{\mu\nu}$ and the orbital part $L^{\mu\nu} = M^{\mu\nu} - S^{\mu\nu}$. And we have shown that the intrinsic part is that part which in the CG system survives and there (as well as in the rest system) has only three components S^{23}, S^{31}, S^{12} different from zero. They can be used to define a new (and different) quantity—the four-vector $(S^{\mu})_R = (0,S^{23},S^{31},S^{12})_R$—and this four-vector is identical to the polarization four-vector (defined earlier) as well as to the S^{μ} defined by Eq. (9-47). There is one restriction, however: This is only true for one single particle with spin.

C. A System of Particles with Spin

We shall now loosen this restriction somewhat by going one step further and considering a system of spinning particles with each having a

$$\begin{aligned} &\text{momentum } p \\ &\text{mass } m = \sqrt{p^{\mu}p_{\mu}} \\ &\text{coordinate } x^{\mu} \\ &\text{total angular momentum } M^{\mu\nu} = x^{\mu}p^{\nu} - x^{\nu}p^{\mu} + S^{\mu\nu} \end{aligned} \qquad (9\text{-}51)$$

We must, however, forget that the spinning particle was obtained from a system of spinless particles by a limiting process and consider the properties in (9-51) as those of a particle with true spin.

Suppose we have now a system of N such spinning particles (with an index $i = 1 \cdots N$ labeling them) and let us consider the total angular momentum of that system:

$$M^{\mu\nu} = \sum_i M_i^{\mu\nu} = \sum_i \left(x_i^{\mu}p_i^{\nu} - x_i^{\nu}p_i^{\mu} + S_i^{\mu\nu}\right) \qquad (9\text{-}52)$$

This can be written in two parts, namely,

$$M^{\mu\nu} = \sum_i L_i^{\mu\nu} + \sum_i S_i^{\mu\nu}$$

but this does in general amount to nothing because we are not able to disentagle these two parts unless we know the state of motion of each particle separately. Why? The answer comes from our previous considerations on a system of particles. Namely, we can go step by step from Eq. (9-37) to Eq. (9-50), but applying everything to the part

$$\sum_i L_i^{\mu\nu} = \sum_i (x^\mu p^\nu - x^\nu p^\mu)_i$$

only. The result is that already $\Sigma_i L_i^{\mu\nu}$ splits into two terms:

$$\sum_i L_i^{\mu\nu} \equiv L^{\mu\nu} + S_{\text{orbit}}^{\mu\nu} = X^\mu P^\nu - X^\nu P^\mu + S_{\text{orbit}}^{\mu\nu}$$

where $S_{\text{orbit}}^{\mu\nu}$ is that part of $M^{\mu\nu}$ which comes from the orbital motion of the particles relative to the center of gravity X but which does not contain contributions from the spins of the particles. It is, however, also an intrinsic angular momentum of our system, although only a part of it. Therefore,

$$\begin{aligned} M^{\mu\nu} &= \sum_i L_i^{\mu\nu} + \sum_i S_i^{\mu\nu} \\ &= X^\mu P^\nu - X^\nu P^\mu + \left[S_{\text{orbit}}^{\mu\nu} + S_{\text{spin}}^{\mu\nu}\right] \end{aligned} \tag{9-53}$$

where

$$\sum_i S_i^{\mu\nu} = S_{\text{spin}}^{\mu\nu}$$

We see that the intrinsic angular momentum is now

$$S^{\mu\nu} = \left[S^{\mu\nu}_{\text{orbit}} + S^{\mu\nu}_{\text{spin}}\right]$$

$$= M^{\mu\nu} - \left(X^{\mu}P^{\nu} - X^{\nu}P^{\mu}\right) = M^{\mu\nu} - L^{\mu\nu} \tag{9-54}$$

If we consider the system as a whole, then $M^{\mu\nu}$, X^{μ}, P^{μ} are known and therefore $\left[S^{\mu\nu}_{\text{orbit}} + S^{\mu\nu}_{\text{spin}}\right]$ can be defined in a covariant way, but not $S^{\mu\nu}_{\text{spin}}$ separately. For that it would be necessary to know $S^{\mu\nu}_{\text{orbit}}$, but this requires the knowledge of each x^{μ}_{i} and p^{μ}_{i} $(i = 1 \cdots N)$. Separating covariantly the true "spin part" $S^{\mu\nu}_{\text{spin}}$ off from the angular momentum $M^{\mu\nu}$ of a system means of course to accomplish this separation in using only the four-vectors and tensors $M^{\mu\nu}$, P^{μ}, X^{μ} pertaining to the system as a whole. In this sense it is not generally possible to define the spin part of a system of particles covariantly.

Our projection operator $\Sigma^{\mu\nu}{}_{\rho\sigma}$ from Eq. (9-50) would fail here even to project out $S^{\mu\nu} = S^{\mu\nu}_{\text{orbit}} + S^{\mu\nu}_{\text{spin}}$. Namely,

$$\Sigma^{\mu\nu}{}_{\rho\sigma}\, M^{\rho\sigma} = \Sigma^{\mu\nu}{}_{\rho\sigma}\, L^{\rho\sigma} + \Sigma^{\mu\nu}{}_{\rho\sigma}\, S^{\rho\sigma}_{\text{orbit}} + \Sigma^{\mu\nu}{}_{\rho\sigma}\, S^{\rho\sigma}_{\text{spin}} \tag{9-55}$$

The first term is zero and the second term equals $S^{\mu\nu}_{\text{orbit}}$, both because of the properties of $\Sigma^{\mu\nu}{}_{\rho\sigma}$ [see after Eq. (9-47) and the derivation of $\Sigma^{\mu\nu}{}_{\rho\sigma}$]. Therefore

$$\Sigma^{\mu\nu}{}_{\rho\sigma}\, M^{\rho\sigma} = S^{\mu\nu}_{\text{orbit}} + \left(\Sigma^{\mu\nu}{}_{\rho\sigma}\, S^{\rho\sigma}_{\text{spin}}\right) \tag{9-56}$$

The last term is, in general, not equal to $S^{\rho\sigma}_{\text{spin}}$. Namely, contracting it with P_{ν} gives

$$\left(\Sigma^{\mu\nu}{}_{\rho\sigma}\, S^{\rho\sigma}_{\text{spin}}\right) P_\nu = 0$$

since $\Sigma^{\mu\nu}{}_{\rho\sigma}\, P_\nu = 0$ [see after Eq. (9-50)].

On the other hand, since $S^{\mu\nu}_{\text{spin}} = \Sigma_i\, S^{\mu\nu}_i$, we have

$$S^{\mu\nu}_{\text{spin}}\, P_\nu = \left(\sum_i S^{\mu\nu}_i\right) P_\nu \neq \sum_i S^{\mu\nu}_i\, P_{i,\nu} = 0 \tag{9-57}$$

Therefore in general

$$\Sigma^{\mu\nu}{}_{\rho\sigma}\, S^{\rho\sigma}_{\text{spin}} \neq S^{\mu\nu}_{\text{spin}}$$

$$\Sigma^{\mu\nu}{}_{\rho\sigma}\, M^{\rho\sigma} \neq S^{\mu\nu} \tag{9-58}$$

$$S^{\mu\nu} P_\nu \neq 0$$

The reason for all this is that it is essential that a Lorentz system exists in which all time components of $M^{\mu\nu}$ vanish. [This is so because the operation

$$W^\mu = \tfrac{1}{2}\, \varepsilon^{\mu}{}_{\nu\rho\sigma}\, P^\nu S^{\rho\sigma}$$

has in the rest system the effect of annihilating the time component see (9-48). This is, of course, permissible only if they are zero anyway. If not, then the following operation $(1/m^2)\, \varepsilon^{\mu\nu}{}_{\rho\sigma}\, P^\rho W^\sigma$, which cannot repair the damage made to $S^{\rho\sigma}$, will not restore the old quantity.] Such a system could be shown to exist in our consider ation of a system of N spinless particles; it was the center of gravi system. However, in a system of n spinning particles, no such system exists in general; writing, namely,

$$M^{\mu\nu} = L^{\mu\nu} + S^{\mu\nu}_{\text{orbit}} + S^{\mu\nu}_{\text{spin}}$$

one sees that one can achieve $L^{\mu\nu} = 0$ and $S^{ok}_{\text{orbit}} = 0$ by going to the CG system. But in that system $\left(S^{\mu\nu}_{\text{spin}}\right)_{CG}$ will, in general, have time components because

$$\left(S^{\mu\nu}_{\text{spin}}\right)_{CG} = \sum_{j=1}^{N} \left(S^{\mu\nu}_j\right)_{CG}$$

and the individual $\left(S^{\mu\nu}_j\right)_{CG}$ have time components. Namely, the time components of the $S^{\mu\nu}_j$ vanish only in the individual rest system R_j of the particle j and the value $\left(S^{\mu\nu}_j\right)_{CG}$ is obtained from $\left(S^{\mu\nu}_j\right)_{R_j}$ by a Lorentz transformation to the CG system—by which time components are generated. As each particle has then, in general, its own Lorentz transformation, there is no hope that in

$$\sum_{j=1}^{N} \left(S^{\mu\nu}_j\right)_{CG}$$

these time components should cancel; this is expressed by Eq. (9-57). Therefore there is in general no Lorentz system in which the time components of $M^{\mu\nu}$ are zero and therefore our procedure does not work.† This is a consequence of considering the $S^{\mu\nu}_i$ as the true spin, which cannot be reduced to an expression of the form

---

† This is, by the way, the reason why one cannot (in general) describe the magnetic field by a four vector: there does not necessarily exist a system where all components of the electric field (= the time component $F^{\mu\nu}$) vanish.

$$\xi_i^\mu \pi_i^\nu - \xi_i^\nu \pi_i^\mu$$

over the internal coordinates ξ_i^μ and momenta π_i^μ of the particle. Otherwise, of course, we could consider this as a cluster of spinless particles again, sum in the old way over all particles of all clusters, and have the old situation in which, as we know, the projection operator works.

It seems therefore that everything we have achieved breaks down if we consider a system of spinning particles.

Luckily enough, there is an exception: it still works if we know the individual momenta of all N particles. This happens in two most important cases:

(a) If only very few particles are present, e.g., in the decay $M \to m + \mu$ or similar situation

(b) If we have a beam of like particles with equal sharp momentum then we know in fact the individual momenta and they all are equal. Therefore in the rest system $\left(S_{\text{orbit}}^{\mu\nu}\right)_R = 0$ because there all particles are at rest and no orbital motion around the origin remains. Finally, as all particles are at rest, also the individual $S_j^{\mu\nu}$ have no time components and thus their sum $\left(\Sigma_j\, S_j^{\mu\nu}\right)_R$ has no time components either. Hence in the rest system

$$\left(M^{\mu\nu}\right)_R = \left(L^{\mu\nu}\right)_R + \left(S_{\text{spin}}^{\mu\nu}\right)_R$$

$$= \left(L^{\mu\nu}\right)_R + \left(\sum_j S_j^{\mu\nu}\right)_R$$

and, by a general Lorentz transformation,

$$M^{\mu\nu} = L^{\mu\nu} + S_{\text{spin}}^{\mu\nu} \tag{9-59}$$

($S_{\text{orbit}}^{\mu\nu} = 0$ holds in every Lorentz system, since it is true in the rest system.) Indeed, our projection operators work here:

$$\left.\begin{array}{ll}\text{(a)} & S^{\mu\nu}_{\text{spin}}\, P_\nu = N \sum_j S^{\mu\nu}_j \; p_\nu = 0 \\ & \text{because the particle's momenta are equal:} \\ & p_\nu = \dfrac{P_\nu}{N} \qquad \text{and} \qquad S^{\mu\nu}_j \, p_\nu = 0 \\ \text{(b)} & \Sigma^{\mu\nu}{}_{\rho\sigma}\, M^{\rho\sigma} = S^{\mu\nu}_{\text{spin}} \\ & \text{This is true because the } P^\nu \text{ in the projection operator can be written } N\cdot p^\nu. \end{array}\right\} \qquad (9\text{-}60)$$

Then $\Sigma^{\mu\nu}{}_{\rho\sigma}$ as a whole annihilates the $L^{\mu\nu}$ part of $M^{\mu\nu}$ and, when it is written as [see (9-50)]

$$\Sigma^{\mu\nu}{}_{\rho\sigma} = \frac{1}{2N^2 m^2}\, \varepsilon^{\mu\nu}{}_{\alpha\beta}\, \varepsilon^{\beta}{}_{\lambda\rho\sigma}\, p^\alpha p^\lambda$$

it clearly reproduces each individual $S^{\mu\nu}_j$ and thus also $S^{\mu\nu}_{\text{spin}} = \Sigma_j S^{\mu\nu}_j$.

This shows that in the important case of a well-defined beam of like particles (or else for a plane-wave state describing a spinning particle) it is indeed possible to separate in a covariant way the true spin part $S^{\mu\nu}_{\text{spin}}$ of the total angular momentum from the $L^{\mu\nu}$ part. In this case $S^{\mu\nu}$ and $W^\mu = mS^\mu$ as defined by Eqs. (9-50) and (9-47), respectively, can likewise be used to describe the state of polarization of the beam. Then S^μ and W^μ are identical with the quantities defined in Sections 9-3 and 9-5 [e.g., Eqs. (9-22) and (9-35)]. It should be stressed that neither $L^{\mu\nu}$ nor $S^{\mu\nu}_{\text{spin}}$ is conserved, but only $M^{\mu\nu}$.

Since a beam of like particles with sharp momentum is described in quantum mechanics as a plane-wave state, we expect also a close relation between $S^{\mu\nu}$ and S^μ and quantum mechanical operators.

We shall establish this relation for the case of Dirac particles (for details, see, e.g., J. Schweber, *Relativistic Quantum Field Theory,* 1961, pp. 74-85. In the same book, pp. 18-53, one also finds furthe information about our polarization four-vector W^{μ}, whose operator counterpart plays an essential role in the classification of the representations of the Lorentz group and thus in the classification of all possible types of relativistic free fields).

9-7 THE CORRESPONDENCE BETWEEN THE POLARIZATION FOUR-VECTOR, ANGULAR MOMENTUM, AND γ-MATRICES IN DIRAC'S THEORY

We choose that particular representation of the γ relation

$$\gamma^{\mu}\gamma^{\nu} + \gamma^{\nu}\gamma^{\mu} = 2g^{\mu\nu} \tag{9-61}$$

in which the components of the spinors split in a natural way into two large and two small ones in the nonrelativistic limit:

$$\gamma^{0} = \gamma_{0} = \begin{pmatrix} 1 & 0 \\ 0 & -1 \end{pmatrix} \qquad \gamma^{k} = -\gamma_{k} = \begin{pmatrix} 0 & \sigma^{k} \\ -\sigma^{k} & 0 \end{pmatrix}$$

$$\gamma^{5} = -\gamma_{5} = i\begin{pmatrix} 0 & 1 \\ 1 & 0 \end{pmatrix}$$

$$\sigma^{1} = \begin{pmatrix} 0 & 1 \\ 1 & 0 \end{pmatrix} \qquad \sigma^{2} = \begin{pmatrix} 0 & -i \\ i & 0 \end{pmatrix} \tag{9-62}$$

$$\sigma^{3} = \begin{pmatrix} 1 & 0 \\ 0 & -1 \end{pmatrix}$$

where the γ's are of course 4×4 matrices, the σ's are $2 \times$ In this particular representation, one obtains for free particl the spinors

$$\psi(x) = e^{-ipx}U(p)$$

$$U(p) = \begin{pmatrix} u_1 \\ u_2 \\ u_3 \\ u_4 \end{pmatrix} \tag{9-63}$$

$$\begin{pmatrix} u_3 \\ u_4 \end{pmatrix} = \frac{\sigma p}{E + m}\begin{pmatrix} u_1 \\ u_2 \end{pmatrix}$$

here $u_1(p)$ and $u_2(p)$ are arbitrary. Obviously $\begin{pmatrix} u_3 \\ u_4 \end{pmatrix}$ vanishes if $\rightarrow 0$.

We now consider two classes of operators

$$\Sigma^{\mu} \equiv i\gamma^5\gamma^{\mu}$$
$$\sigma^{\mu\nu} \equiv \frac{i}{2}(\gamma^{\mu}\gamma^{\nu} - \gamma^{\nu}\gamma^{\mu}) \tag{9-64}$$

ne shows easily, by means of (9-62), that

$$\Sigma^0 = \begin{pmatrix} 0 & 1 \\ -1 & 0 \end{pmatrix} \qquad \Sigma^k = \begin{pmatrix} \sigma^k & 0 \\ 0 & -\sigma^k \end{pmatrix}$$
$$\sigma^{ok} = i\begin{pmatrix} 0 & \sigma^k \\ \sigma^k & 0 \end{pmatrix} \qquad \sigma^{jk} = \begin{pmatrix} \sigma^{\ell} & 0 \\ 0 & \sigma^{\ell} \end{pmatrix} \quad (jk\ell \text{ cycl.}) \tag{9-65}$$

e define now

$$S^{\mu} \equiv \langle \Sigma^{\mu} \rangle \equiv \overline{\psi}\, i\gamma^5\gamma^{\mu}\psi \qquad \overline{\psi} \equiv \psi^*\gamma^0$$
$$S^{\mu\nu} \equiv \langle \sigma^{\mu\nu} \rangle \equiv \overline{\psi}\,\frac{i}{2}(\gamma^{\mu}\gamma^{\nu} - \gamma^{\nu}\gamma^{\mu})\psi \tag{9-66}$$

nd show that they are identical with our old S^{μ} and $S^{\mu\nu}$, respec- vely. Since the above expressions are manifestly covariant, we ly need to check the assertion in the rest system, where u_3 = $= 0$.

Since, according to (9-65) Σ^0 and σ^{0k} both interchange $\begin{pmatrix} u_1 \\ u_2 \end{pmatrix}$ wit $\begin{pmatrix} u_3 \\ u_4 \end{pmatrix}$, we have

$$\langle \Sigma^0 \rangle_R = \langle \sigma^{0k} \rangle_R = 0$$

Furthermore Σ^k and σ^{jk} do not interchange $\begin{pmatrix} u_1 \\ u_2 \end{pmatrix}$ with $\begin{pmatrix} u_3 \\ u_4 \end{pmatrix}$; thus

$$\langle \Sigma^k \rangle_R = (u_1^* u_2^*) \sigma^k \begin{pmatrix} u_1 \\ u_2 \end{pmatrix} = \langle \sigma^k \rangle_R$$

$$\langle \sigma^{jk} \rangle_R = (u_1^* u_2^*) \sigma^\ell \begin{pmatrix} u_1 \\ u_2 \end{pmatrix} = \langle \sigma^\ell \rangle_R \qquad (jk\ell \text{ cycl.})$$

Hence

$$(S^\mu)_R = (0, \langle \sigma \rangle)_R$$

$$(S^{\mu\nu})_R = \left\{ \begin{matrix} \langle \sigma^{0k} \rangle = 0 \\ \langle \sigma^{jk} \rangle = \langle \sigma \rangle \end{matrix} \right\}_R \tag{9-67}$$

That is, in the rest system S^μ and $S^{\mu\nu}$ reduce (in a loose sense) to our old quantities. Therefore this is true in all Lorentz systems and we have established the correspondence

$$S^{\mu\nu} \longleftrightarrow \sigma^{\mu\nu} = \frac{i}{2}(\gamma^\mu \gamma^\nu - \gamma^\nu \gamma^\mu)$$

$$S^\mu \longleftrightarrow \Sigma^\mu = i\gamma^5 \gamma^\mu \tag{9-68}$$

Equation (9-67) also shows that the assertion that for the true spin the relation $S^{\mu\nu} P_\nu = 0$ holds is at least fulfilled for spin $\frac{1}{2}$ particles.

The operator Σ^μ is closely related to a covariant projection operator P_t with the property that for any spinor ψ, the projected spinor

$$\psi_t \equiv P_t \psi \tag{9-69}$$

has the expectation value of the spin pointing in the direction **t**, namely,

$$\langle \sigma^{23}, \sigma^{31}, \sigma^{12} \rangle$$

parallel to **t**. Here t is a four-vector,

$$t^{\mu} = (t^{0}, \mathbf{t}) \tag{9-70}$$

whose zero component is chosen such that

$$p^{\mu} t_{\mu} = 0 \tag{9-71}$$

The projection operator then assumes the form

$$P_t = \tfrac{1}{2} \; 1 + \Sigma^{\mu} \; t_{\mu} \frac{E}{|E|} \tag{9-72}$$

For further information see Hamilton, *The Theory of Elementary Particles*, 1959, pp. 124-129.

INDEX